OLIVER CROMWELL

and the

Puritan Revolution

is one of the volumes
in the

TEACH YOURSELF HISTORY
LIBRARY

Edited by A. L. ROWSE

Teach Yourself History

VOLUMES READY OR IN PREPARATION

The Use of History, by A. L. Rowse
Pericles and Athens, by A. R. Burn
Alexander the Great and the Hellenistic Empire, by A. R. Burn
Agricola and Roman Britain, by A. R. Burn
Constantine and the Conversion of Europe, by A. H. M. Jones
Charlemagne and Western Europe, by H. St. L. B. Moss
Wycliffe and the Beginnings of English Nonconformity, by K. B. McFarlane
Henry V and the Invasion of France, by E. F. Jacob
Joan of Arc and the Recovery of France, by Alice Buchan
Lorenzo dei Medici and Renaissance Italy, by C. M. Ady
Machiavelli and Renaissance Italy, by John Hale
Erasmus and the Northern Renaissance, by Margaret Mann Phillips
Thomas Cromwell and the English Reformation, by A. G. Dickens
Cranmer and the English Reformation by F. E. Hutchinson
Elizabeth I and Tudor England, by J. Hurstfield
Whitgift and the English Church, by V. J. K. Brook
Raleigh and the British Empire, by D. B. Quinn
Richelieu and the French Monarchy, by C. V. Wedgwood
Oliver Cromwell and the Puritan Revolution, by Maurice Ashley
Milton and the English Mind, by F. E. Hutchinson
Louis XIV and the Greatness of France, by Maurice Ashley
Peter the Great and the Emergence of Russia, by B. H. Sumner
Chatham and the British Empire, by Sir Charles Grant Robertson
Cook and the Opening of the Pacific, by James A. Williamson
Catherine the Great and the Expansion of Russia, by Gladys Scott Thomson
Benjamin Franklin and the American People, by Esmond Wright
Warren Hastings and British India, by Penderel Moon
Washington and the American Revolution, by Esmond Wright
Robespierre and the French Revolution, by J. M. Thompson
Napoleon and the Awakening of Europe, by Felix Markham
Bolivar and the Independence of Spanish America, by J. B. Trend
Jefferson and American Democracy, by Max Beloff
Pushkin and Russian Literature, by Janko Lavrin
Marx, Proudhon and European Socialism, by J. Hampden Jackson
Abraham Lincoln and the United States, by K. C. Wheare
Napoleon III and the Second Empire, by J. P. T. Bury
Alexander II and the Modernisation of Russia, by W. E. Mosse
Gladstone and Liberalism, by J. L. Hammond and M. R. D. Foot
Livingstone and Africa, by Jack Simmons
Clemenceau and the Third Republic, by J. Hampden Jackson
Woodrow Wilson and American Liberalism, by E. M. Hugh-Jones
Lenin and the Russian Revolution, by Christopher Hill
Botha, Smuts and South Africa, by Basil Williams
Roosevelt and Modern America, by J. A. Woods

OLIVER CROMWELL

and the

Puritan Revolution

by
MAURICE ASHLEY

THE ENGLISH UNIVERSITIES PRESS LTD
102, Newgate Street
LONDON, E.C.1

First Printed   1958

PRINTED AND BOUND IN ENGLAND
FOR THE ENGLISH UNIVERSITIES PRESS LTD.,
BY HAZELL WATSON AND VINEY LTD., AYLESBURY

53373

Contents

A General Introduction
to the Series

THIS series has been undertaken in the conviction that there can be no subject of study more important than history. Great as have been the conquests of natural science in our time—such that many think of ours as a scientific age *par excellence*—it is even more urgent and necessary that advances should be made in the social sciences if we are to gain control of the forces of nature loosed upon us. The bed out of which all the social sciences spring is history; there they find, in greater or lesser degree, subject-matter and material verification or contradiction.

There is no end to what we can learn from history, if only we will, for it is coterminous with life. Its special field is the life of man in society, and at every point we can learn vicariously from the experience of others before us in history.

To make one point only—the understanding of politics : how can we hope to understand the world of affairs around us if we do not know how it came to be what it is? How to understand Germany, or Soviet Russia, or the United States, or ourselves—without knowing something of their history?

There is no subject that is more useful or, indeed, indispensable.

Some evidence of the growing awareness of this may be seen in the immense increase in the interest of the reading public in history and the much larger place the subject has come to take in education in our time.

This series has been planned to meet the needs and demands of a very wide public and of education—they are indeed the same. I am convinced that the most congenial, as well as the most concrete and practical, approach to history is the biographical, through the lives of the great men whose actions have been so much part of history and whose careers in turn have been so moulded and formed by events.

The key idea of this series, and what distinguishes it from any other that has appeared, is the intention by way of a biography of a great man to open up a significant historical theme; for example, Cromwell and the Puritan Revolution, or Lenin and the Russian Revolution.

My hope is, in the end, as the series fills out and completes itself, by a sufficient number of biographies to cover whole periods and subjects in that way. To give you the history of the United States, for example, or the British Empire or France, *via* a number of biographies of their leading historical figures.

That should be something new, as well as convenient and practical, in education.

I need hardly say that I am a strong believer in people with good academic standards writing once more for the general reading public, and of the public being given the best that the universities can provide. From this point of view this series is intended to bring the university into the homes of the people.

A. L. ROWSE.

ALL SOULS COLLEGE,
OXFORD.

Foreword

THE aim of the present book is to describe what the Puritan Revolution achieved and to explain Oliver Cromwell's contribution to it. My intention has been to provide a clear and succinct narrative and to paint my picture upon a broad canvas, which finds room for Queen Elizabeth I as well as King Charles II. For a different and fuller appraisal of Cromwell's life and work, readers may care to turn to *The Greatness of Oliver Cromwell,* published in 1957. Most reviewers seem to have thought that I satisfactorily established the nature of Cromwell's greatness, though one or two could not be shaken from their conviction that he was a hypocrite. So many men, so many opinions. But I have taken notice of some criticisms in this book. I only hope that I succeed in what I set out to do here : to enable those who wish to learn about one of the most revealing epochs in the story of the British people to teach themselves its history.

MAURICE ASHLEY.

Chapter One

An Elizabethan

ON 24 March 1603 Queen Elizabeth I "of famous memory"—"We need not be ashamed to call her so", as Oliver Cromwell once said—went the way of all flesh. She had received the last ministrations of the Church of England from her "little black husband", John Whitgift, the Archbishop of Canterbury, who, at her command, had chastised but not crushed the rising English Puritans. During her final days upon earth the seventy-year old Queen, ruler of England for more than forty-five years and proven mistress of her realm, had lain pensive and silent in her palace. Like Oliver Cromwell when he came to die two generations later, she had no wish to eat or to drink, but to make what haste she could to be gone. It was clear to contemporaries, as it has become to posterity, that an epoch in English history was ending.

Four years earlier, on 25 April 1599, a son had been born to a modest country gentleman named Robert Cromwell and to his wife Elizabeth in the county town of Huntingdon, a son whom they named Oliver after his rich uncle. Thus Oliver Cromwell, like William Shakespeare, was an Elizabethan, and was brought up to learn in his youth, while the first of the Stuarts were reigning, about the splendid and exciting times when England had established herself as a great Protestant Power in Europe, when English adventurers began to sail distant oceans in search of fabulous plunder, and when Sir Francis Drake had "singed the beard" of the King of Spain.

Not that those Elizabethan days had been free from many dangers and anxieties. In the opinion of not a few of her subjects and of all her foreign enemies, Queen Elizabeth I was illegitimate, a bastard and a heretic, the un-

wanted daughter of Anne Boleyn, the Queen whose
execution had been ordered by her husband on a charge of
adultery. In the wild areas of the north, rebellions had
more than once been plotted against the Virgin Queen;
an alliance between Spain and Scotland had been adumbrated to thrust her from her throne and replace her by her
Roman Catholic rival, Mary Queen of Scots, claiming
descent from the founder of the Tudor dynasty. From foes
abroad came the boast that 20,000 English Roman Catholics would, upon a given signal, rise against the Queen of
England for the sake of the old religion. For had not Pope
Pius V in 1570 published a Bull deposing her from her
throne? Gregory XIII, who succeeded Pius V in the papal
see, welcomed the notion of assassinating the English
Queen. Assassination was a fashionable political weapon
of the day (Queen Elizabeth herself preferred the idea of
Mary Queen of Scots being put to death by her gaoler to
ordering her public execution); in August 1572 thousands
of French Protestants were massacred by royal command
on St. Bartholomew's Day, and in June 1584, at a second
attempt, Prince William of Orange, the Protestant hero of
the Dutch, was murdered. Two years later the Pope
offered a million crowns to King Philip II of Spain if he
were to carry out a successful invasion of England.

Meanwhile, soon after Queen Elizabeth came to the
throne, an English college had been set up at Douai to train
missionary priests for the reconversion of England. In 1580
the Society of Jesus took the task in hand, and Jesuits
daringly flitted to and fro from the Continent, hiding with
sympathizers in nearly every county and creating alarm
upon all sides. The Queen's government retorted by
making it high treason for any of her subjects to withdraw
from the Church of England to Rome, and by imposing a
crippling fine of £20 a month for failure to attend Anglican services. Thus both cross and sword were raised aloft
to destroy Elizabethan England.

Gradually but inexorably the country had been committed to the Protestant cause in Europe. In the fifteen-
sixties Queen Elizabeth promised aid to the French
Huguenots; in 1585 she made a treaty with the men of the

Dutch Netherlands in revolt against the Spanish Empire. Her favourite, the Earl of Leicester, left with an army for The Hague, and Sir Francis Drake scoured the world "beyond the line" to seize Spanish treasure. War against Spain followed, and it was prolonged years after the resounding defeat of the Armada in the summer of 1588. In June 1596, another of the Queen's favourites, the first Earl of Essex, sacked the city of Cadiz. Efforts were exerted by English forces to procure a foothold on the continental mainland so as to neutralize Spanish plans to invade England from what is now Belgium. Thus there arose, largely in response to Catholic revolutionary plotting, directed from Rome and Madrid, a foreign policy of anti-Spanish character, sustained by naval might, supported by expeditions to the Low Countries, and buttressed by general aid and encouragement to European Protestants. That, too, was to be, by and large, the foreign policy of Oliver Cromwell.

Queen Elizabeth I insisted that foreign policy, like matters of religion (she had been made Supreme Governor of the Church of England by the Act of Uniformity in 1559), was the sole concern of the Crown. Nevertheless, she needed the assistance of her parliaments, who granted her subsidies for her war against Spain. She, for her part, continued the policy first pursued by her father, King Henry VIII, of employing the House of Commons to strengthen the monarchy. The peerage was now kept in its place, and some great men who sullied their honour by plotting against the Queen were executed. In the Commons the Queen's policy was represented by a group of capable Privy Councillors, men like William Cecil and his son Robert, Sir Francis Walsingham and Sir Christopher Hatton, who handled their fellow members with tact and skill, and while invoking their patriotism, under the Queen's orders, prevented the House from trespassing upon the royal prerogatives—the traditional rights of the Throne.

But the early parliaments of Queen Elizabeth's reign were both obstreperous and critical, and before she died the Queen had received her fill of them. It was under pres-

sure from her first House of Commons that a Protestant
settlement had been quickly effected after "Bloody
Mary's" death. In the Commons of 1563 a Puritan group
of some forty-five members caused its influence to be felt
at Court. As Elizabeth learned the craft of kingship, as the
realities of the threats from abroad became obvious, and
when the war with Spain broke out in the fifteen-eighties,
the Commons became a little more pliable. Yet Puritan
leaders, like the two Wentworth brothers, had arisen to
challenge the government's policies, and claims for freedom from arrest and freedom of speech for members of
parliament were regularly asserted. During the reign of
Queen Elizabeth I, questions of parliamentary procedure
were settled. But the Queen never yielded over what she
deemed to be matters of royal prerogative. She had members arrested, or "sequestered", if they stepped out of
bounds; she qualified their freedom of speech; she addressed the members of her Lower House with supreme
artistry and graciousness; but she ruled them with an iron
hand in a velvet glove. Still, under the shadow of her
throne, London was a restless, eager, energetic centre of
political activity, expanding trade, religious agitation, and
artistic endeavour, and Westminster lay close to the heart
of it all. By the end of the reign the Commons were beginning to show signs of winning the initiative in legislation,
were still striving to make their views felt about matters of
high policy, and never fully abandoning their prolonged
attempts to reshape the religious practices of the nation.

The House of Commons was then composed chiefly of
landed gentry. It was accepted by all as an institution that
conferred social prestige. The aim of any distinguished
commoner was to go to Westminster as the premier knight
of his shire. Although the Queen enfranchised over thirty
boroughs during her reign, the country gentlemen invaded
these boroughs and probably not more than fifty members
out of a House of 460 were merchants or tradesmen. In
spite of the wider openings for foreign trade created as a
result of adventuring abroad, England was still, when
Queen Elizabeth I died, essentially an agricultural
country, and fortunes were acquired by rising families by

means of astutely arranged marriage settlements, by growing wool for cloth upon a large scale, by trade or the practice of the law, or by obtaining grants of office through
royal advisers and favourites. In the counties the people
were ruled by Lords-Lieutenant first established by the
Tudors, by the sheriffs who organized and frequently
manipulated the elections to parliament, and, above all,
by Justices of the Peace who met at quarter sessions and
were responsible for enforcing Acts of parliament and
managing social affairs. In those days when communications were primitive, roads poor, and regular postal services almost non-existent, the government was mainly dependent upon the voluntary co-operation of the local
magnates and gentry for effective administration. Every
ruler in Whitehall, at a time when neither a police force
nor a standing army existed, had either to bow to the
wishes of the local magnates or to find some extraordinary
means (as Cromwell was to do later with his major-
generals) of maintaining the authority of the central
government over the English provinces.

To parliament came, whenever they were summoned,
these leading local gentry—the Lords-Lieutenants to the
House of Lords, many of the J.P.s to the House of Commons—to give expression to their grievances, to approve
legislation, and reluctantly to vote taxation. Without their
goodwill the Queen could neither enforce order at home
nor wage war abroad. Even then she could hardly make
ends meet. Careful, even parsimonious, as she was, she was
compelled to sell part of the Crown lands to help pay for
her armies and fleets. It was obvious that if her successor
was a married man with extravagant tastes and lacking
her acquired skill in the handling of parliaments, these
English gentlemen who gathered periodically from the
shires and boroughs, assertive and conscious of their
strength, would exercise a growing influence upon national
policy. It was to these gentry—an expanding middle class
—that Oliver Cromwell belonged.

Though, on the surface at least, the country appeared to
be peaceably settled while Oliver Cromwell was a small
child—King James I, when he came down from Scotland,

held the most optimistic opinions about his prospects in a richer kingdom—the economic outlook was more doubtful. A depression occurred as the Spanish war waned, and the last years of Queen Elizabeth I's reign were clouded by bad harvests and by recurrent plagues. Prices were rising in consequence of the inflow of silver from South America to Europe, but, owing to the commonness of long leases, rents did not necessarily rise with prices, and the smaller landowners suffered. But landowners who had accumulated capital or proved themselves to be businesslike managers of their estates did well enough—the Spencers of Northamptonshire were examples of this prospering class—but smaller men without capital or other sources of income than rents or who were extravagant spenders, soon found themselves in trouble. On the whole, however, though families rose and fell in the scale of wealth, as at any other time in English history, the general picture is one of a thriving upper and middle class. After all, much of the wealth of the Church had been redistributed among the laity in consequence of the Reformation, and had fructified in their hands. Big fortunes were being built in the City of London, where trade, industries, crafts, and money-lending flourished.

The population of England and Wales was only about five million, out of whom a quarter was concentrated in the Home Counties and perhaps one-twelfth in London itself. A few hundred wealthy families were, under the Queen, the real power in the nation. In most counties there were a few important families which acquired a virtually prescriptive right to direct local government and represent their neighbours and dependants at Westminster. In Huntingdonshire the Cromwells were, in Queen Elizabeth I's reign, unquestionably the dominant family. But this was not a caste system. The gentry intermarried with lawyers, with other professional men, and with merchants, all of whom could earn an excellent living. Younger sons of landed families were often apprenticed and became in their turn important men in the city. The contrast between rich and poor was marked. Whereas peers of the realm might obtain a large income from lands and offices, the day labourer would be lucky to earn eightpence a day. On the coat-tails of the well-to-do hung the small landlords and hard-working farmers with incomes in the £300- to £500-a-year bracket. To that class Robert Cromwell, father of Oliver, belonged.

The gulf between rich and poor was to be observed among the clergy as well as among the laity. The bishops, it is true, had lost social status as a result of the Reformation, and had been transformed from feudal landlords into paid administrators. Since they held their properties only for their lives, they had little impulse to be improving landlords; they generally had, in effect, to pay for their appointments, and as Queen Elizabeth was "the supreme plunderer of the Church", they were obliged to look after their material interests as best they could. Pluralism and nepotism were frequent. Most of the higher clergy held offices to which they never attended in person. One bishop used the fines, which he was entitled to exact when his leases fell in, to provide portions for his nieces whom he married to clergy and on whom he conferred preferments in his diocese; another bishop is said to have leased episcopal manors to his wife, children, sisters, and cousins. The Bishop of Durham still claimed feudal dues on a medieval scale. The Archbishops of Canterbury and York enjoyed substantial incomes, and when John Whitgift was Archbishop of Canterbury he had a big retinue and an armoury capable of equipping a troop of cavalry.

The parish clergy, on the other hand, were for the most part very poorly paid, many of them hardly above the level of subsistence. "Some are so poor", it was said, "that they cannot attend their ministry, but are fain to keep schools, nay ale-houses, some of them." No wonder the bishops were disliked by many lower clergy. Vicars were usually dependent upon pittances from lay patrons who had acquired the tithes, and although Archbishop Whitgift and King James I tried to increase their incomes, the clergy as a whole were extremely badly off, of a low standard of education, and suffered every temptation to scamp their duties.

Although Puritanism in due course was to become a

rabidly anti-episcopalian movement, it was less the wealth or corruption of the Elizabethan bishops than the ignorance and idleness of many of the lower clergy that provoked the early ardours of those who dedicated themselves to purifying the Church. Some of the first Puritans were keen to substitute nation-wide preaching of an evangelical and stimulating character for the set services of the Elizabethan Church; they wanted to press further the anti-ritualistic tendencies represented by the prayer-book of 1552, getting rid of such remaining Roman Catholic ceremonies as the use of the ring in marriage, baptism at the font, or communion at the altar. Evangelically minded clergy, who had drunk at the fountain of Calvinism in Geneva and were inspired to remodel the entire government of the Church upon a Presbyterian pattern, were in Queen Elizabeth's reign a minority. But all of the Puritans wanted to purge church worship of its traditional Catholic characteristics, and to base its services entirely upon preaching and prayer. The Anglican clergy preached comparatively little, reading to their congregations from time to time prescribed homilies on such acceptable topics as the obligations of wives and the evils of drink. Queen Elizabeth herself disapproved of too many sermons, and was even known to interrupt court preachers with whom she disagreed or who went on too long. The early Puritan movement reached its climax five years after she came to the throne, when a motion for the abolition of all the practices most disliked by the Puritans, including even the wearing of surplices, was defeated in the Lower House of Convocation by only a single vote.

The Queen consistently opposed the Puritan principles from the very beginning of her reign, and she never changed her opinions : she suppressed a movement in the Parliament of 1571 to revise the Prayer Book; she acted rapidly when a temerarious gentleman introduced a Bill in 1587 to adopt the Geneva Prayer Book and abolish the existing government of the Church; she ordered her bishops to repress all the elaborate attempts to convert the Church from within to a kind of Presbyterian establishment. She saw to it that the archbishops, by publishing

18

disciplinary instructions, upheld the middle way between Roman Catholicism and Presbyterianism, which she thought was the path that her Church should follow, a path persuasively mapped out by the "Judicious" Dr. Hooker in his famous book, *The Laws of Ecclesiastical Polity*. The supposed authors and printers of a series of outspoken Puritan tracts known as the "Marprelate Libels" were pursued and arrested. (It is significant that their probable author, who escaped punishment, was a prominent member of parliament.) Professor Thomas Cartwright of Cambridge University, who advocated the full Presbyterian system, was deprived of his Fellowship and went into exile for some years. By the last decade of the reign, because of the unrelenting exertions of the Queen and her Archbishop, the Puritan drive had been checked, but only temporarily.

The Puritans were not distinguished by any differences of theology or doctrine from the rest of the Church. Although some modern writers have attempted to draw fine distinctions, the great majority of the leaders of the English Church in the latter part of Queen Elizabeth I's reign believed in the Calvinistic doctrine of predestination. But granted that this was Christianity, England was a Christian nation under a Christian Queen. Sir John Neale, our leading authority on the reign, has recently re-affirmed his belief in the reality of the Queen's religion; she certainly called upon the name of God often enough in her speeches. All her subjects were Christians, except perhaps for a handful of Crypto-Jews concentrated in the City of London. But within the ruling class in Church and State were nuances of faith : theirs was a flexible religion. Ministers of State like Lord Burghley, the Earl of Leicester, and Sir Francis Walsingham sympathized with the Puritan movement. So did some of the archbishops and bishops so long as their own offices were not attacked. The Thirty-nine Articles of the Church were perfectly susceptible of a variety of interpretations, including a Puritan one. After all, once King Henry VIII had begun the reformation of the Church, why should it stop? But his daughter disliked and fought against what she regarded as the subversive, seditious, and democratic outlook of the Puritan enthusiasts, and she worked persistently against them. Nevertheless, the obvious weaknesses of the Church were not mended, the status of the clergy was not raised, the attacks on ritual were not stilled. The call for Church reform permeated society and proved particularly attractive to the new mercantile and professional classes who were beginning to command influence in the English towns and ports as the new century dawned. By the time that Oliver Cromwell was growing to manhood, Puritanism in a broad sense had already become a significant part of the English social landscape.

In the first half of the seventeenth century England was, as it has never been again since, essentially a Christian country. The large qualities of private letters from the period, which have survived in now decaying country houses and have come down to us in surprisingly legible handwriting, are suffused with a deep, personal, Christian faith. Life on earth, after all, was even shorter than it is now and fraught with extreme perils. If men and women managed to overcome the hazards of youth, including primitive midwifery, childish diseases, and horribly insanitary conditions in towns, especially in the capital, they might still be swept away by smallpox, or bubonic plague, or by illnesses for which there was no known cure. Doctoring was still elementary, consisting chiefly of blood-letting, purges, and fantastic medicines. Even physicians who rose to positions of authority and trust admitted that life was a gamble and might as well be enjoyed as long as it lasted. Consequently, few people were not obsessed with the thought that they were ever at the mercy of an inscrutable Providence, that their fate was determined for them from eternity, and that their only hope of a satisfying peace of mind was to be found in the thought of everlasting happiness in other worlds to come. To eighteenth-century rationalists, as to twentieth-century sceptics, there has seemed something ludicrous and slightly nauseating in Oliver Cromwell's dependence upon providential guidance and in his anxiety over the right Christian approach to questions of politics (it was more understandable to the mid-Victorians), but this, after all, was the accepted and not exceptional approach to life among the men of his own generation and background.

Puritanism, as Dr. Rowse has observed, began as a movement for reform, and became, as such movements do, a campaign for power. In its first stages it did not aim to destroy or even capture the Church, but merely to remould it and rid it of its excrescences. During Queen Elizabeth I's reign, the movement was strong both in the Lower House of Convocation and in the House of Commons. In the reign of King James I funds were raised by well-to-do sympathizers to buy up Church impropriations and benefices so as to impose the appointments of Puritan-minded preachers at key-points within the Church. A former Huguenot church in London was selected as a training centre whence preachers with a radical frame of mind should go forth to evangelize the Church from within. An idea that became popular with Oliver Cromwell was that such Christian "lecturers" should move around the country preaching both in churches and in the open air to offset the "dumb mouths" of the parish incumbents, to arouse congregations from inertia, and to destroy all the relics of popery. But the bishops, alerted by the Elizabethan tradition of scotching all such subversion, could not be by-passed by any ingenious devices of that kind. When King James I, though a new-comer from Presbyterian Scotland, refused to be cajoled into sympathizing with English Puritanism, and when King Charles I, himself a ritualist by instinct, positively rejected it, its advocates were driven on irresistibly towards an open assault upon the bishops, and in the end, sustained a revolution that temporarily overthrew not only the existing Church but also its defender, the monarchy.

No one can hope to understand a revolution without some picture of what went on before. In the long reign of Queen Elizabeth I occurred a movement of the House of Commons towards vigorous independence, the spread of

Puritanism, coupled with discontent over the rule of the Church of England, and, above all, the expansion of an ambitious middle class. That was the inheritance of the Stuarts who for so long had governed the unruly Scots with varying success. That was the background of the coming rebellion against them and of Oliver Cromwell's infancy.

Chapter Two

Farmer and Puritan

AS is the case with earlier great men not born on the steps of the throne, little is known about Oliver Cromwell's youth. More is known about his ancestry. The family's fortune was built upon the dissolution of the monasteries. Oliver's great-great-grandfather, Morgan Williams, came down from Wales with King Henry VII. His son, Richard Williams, was knighted by King Henry VIII, and changed his name to Cromwell in deference to his uncle by marriage, Thomas Cromwell, King Henry VIII's notorious minister who carried through the dissolution of the monasteries. Thus there was a Welsh strain in Cromwell's character on the paternal side. His mother was a Norfolk girl, and the Cromwells, who were a prolific race, settled mainly in Huntingdonshire and Cambridgeshire, though branches of the family were scattered in other counties. As John Buchan wrote, "most of the creative forces of England had gone to the making of him".

The Cromwells were indeed typical of the classes that under the monarchy helped to rule England. In the county where Oliver was born there were only two influential families—the Cromwells of Huntingdon and the Montagus of Kimbolton. They acted as Lords-Lieutenant, or their deputies, sheriffs, Justices of the Peace, commissioners of sewers, and members of parliament. When Oliver's wealthy uncle, the head of the family, was involved in financial difficulties, it was a Montagu who bought up his Tudor mansion at Hinchingbrooke, where Oliver played as a child and may even have met the future King Charles I. When Oliver was first elected a member of parliament for Huntingdon, it was a Montagu who was his fellow-member for the borough. When Oliver went to

Cambridge, he was at a college, Sidney Sussex, of which a Montagu was the first master. Finally, when Cromwell, years later, was appointed a lieutenant-general in the parliamentary army, he acted as second in command to a Montagu whose fortunes had improved as those of the Cromwells declined. It was before the father of this Montagu—Henry, first Earl of Manchester—that Cromwell was hailed when he was concerned in a quarrel over the new charter which had been granted to the borough of Huntingdon in 1631.

Oliver Cromwell himself said once that he was "by birth a gentleman living neither in any considerable height nor yet in obscurity". Some biographers have, none the less, asserted that he was no more than an insignificant squire. But the Cromwells were unquestionably a family that counted in the east of England, and had been important there ever since the time of King Henry VIII. Their fortunes were on the decline when Oliver himself reached manhood—or, at any rate, upon a temporary decline, but they still carried sufficient weight to sustain his election to the House of Commons.

Oliver's father was a younger son and inherited only a small estate; but he, too, had been the county sheriff and an M.P. He was the close friend of Dr. Thomas Beard, the master of the local grammar school where Oliver received his early education, and afterwards his father sent him on to Sidney Sussex. Dr. Beard was an eminent Puritan publicist and Sidney Sussex was a hot-bed of Puritanism; the college was, indeed, founded to train Puritan preachers. Thus Robert Cromwell must have sympathized with the rising Puritan movement (as some of the Montagus did also), and from his family, his teachers, and his friends Oliver imbibed the Puritan approach to life. He read the Authorized Version of the Bible and learned the Psalms by heart; he lived in an age when many religious men, including Dr. Beard himself, were convinced that those were the "latter days" spoken of in the Bible and that the Apocalypse was not far distant. The Lord God, Cromwell was taught, was interested in the most intimate details of men's lives, and punished them if they failed to serve His

24

purposes. What is history, Cromwell once asked, but God revealing Himself? He was to tell one of his sons to read Sir Walter Ralegh's *History of the World*, which would add much more to his understanding than any "fragment of a story". Ralegh interpreted history as the unfolding of the providential purposes and as exemplifying the punishment of the wicked who failed to fulfil them. Dr. Beard taught the same thing. To do God's will was man's destiny. Either he was chosen to be the servant of the Lord or he was a "reprobate" born to sin. Dr. Samuel Ward, the master of Sidney Sussex, during the year which Oliver spent there when he was aged seventeen, adhered to this uncompromising predestinarian view. Anyone who believed in "free will" or "justification by faith", that good doctor of divinity thought, was preaching "the vilest and most feculent points of all popery".

In the summer of 1617 Oliver's father died, and Oliver then seems to have left Cambridge, with his instruction in Calvinist theology cut short. In the course of his education he acquired considerable Latin, and perhaps a little Greek and enough arithmetic to do his accounts; but most of it consisted of Puritan theology and ethics and Puritan history; he never seems to have read much besides the Bible. His other interests were horses and music, in which he indulged when he became Lord Protector. After a short spell at home in Huntingdon he went to London where, like many other country gentlemen of his day, he appears to have acquired a smattering of the Common Law in the Inns of Court. On 22 August 1620 he was married to the daughter of a fur dealer, and again returned to Huntingdon to become an arable farmer. The marriage was no doubt arranged for him by relatives, as was the usual custom of the time. But throughout his career Oliver was blessed with a happy family life. He once wrote to his wife: "Truly if I love thee not too well, I think I err not on the other hand too much. Thou art dearer to me than any creature." He was devoted to his widowed mother, and to his sons and daughters. Two of his sons died in early manhood and another as a baby. Otherwise his was a united family, and his sharp Puritan creed was softened by tolerance and humane understanding. Though he was pierced by the conviction that it was his duty to serve God's purpose in life and to interpret His will, his was a religion based upon love and not upon fear.

Cromwell's "conversion", the usual emotional stage through which the Puritans of his generation passed, does not seem to have taken place until he was twenty-nine, after several of his children had been born, and just before he was first elected to parliament. It was only then, in spite of his Puritan upbringing, that the full impact of his religion struck him. Andrew Marvell wrote in a poem upon the "First Anniversary of the Government under Oliver Cromwell" :

> *"For neither didst thou from the first apply*
> *Thy sober spirit unto things too high,*
> *But in thine own fields exercisedst long*
> *An healthful mind within a body strong."*

His body may have been strong—in a young farmer who loved riding that was to be expected—but there are sufficient scattered pieces of evidence to suggest that in his early married life he was the victim of searing emotions and anxious thoughts, was the subject of alternating periods of depression and exaltation. Like most powerful characters, he had a temper that was easily provoked when he believed that injustices had been done or the will of God defied. When he was a member of the Long Parliament, he attacked the Privy Council for the whipping and imprisoning of an apprentice named John Lilburne in such a violent speech that it impressed itself many years afterwards upon the memories of those who heard it. Towards the end of Cromwell's life his steward remarked on his "fiery temper", though he thought that by then he had learned to "keep it down".

In a man so turbulently built, conversion was an exhausting experience. Cromwell pictured himself as "the chief of sinners" who had "lived in and loved darkness and hated the light". Like John Bunyan and many another seventeenth-century Puritan, he exaggerated the contrast between the iniquities of his past life and the riches of

God's mercy. But from then on he believed that he was one of the "elect", a Christian who shared St. Paul's experience upon the road to Damascus; he acknowledged his call from God to the service of the Christian community.

Cromwell's early married life, punctuated by the frequent birth of children and therefore bringing additional responsibilities, no doubt demanded a re-examination of himself which contributed to his conversion. At first he had a struggle to earn a satisfactory livelihood. Two-thirds of his father's small estate had been assigned to the support of his mother and sisters; although his wife brought him a dowry, it may not have been much. In the early sixteen-twenties the harvests were poor, and later, when they improved, prices were not as good as they had previously been. An arable farmer working upon the medieval strip system could not expect to do much more than make ends meet. In 1627 Oliver's rich uncle abandoned Hinching-brooke, and it was not until 1638, when Cromwell was nearly forty, that he inherited property from a maternal uncle who lived in Ely. Before then he had tried his luck as a grazier at St. Ives. But now, in 1638, he moved again to Ely, where he became a man of substance. After the civil war began, he wrote to a friend that his "estate was little". He wrote this when he was trying to raise money for his soldiers' pay, however, and it would be a mistake to make too much of Cromwell's relative poverty or declining fortunes when he was a younger man. At a pinch he could raise a thousand pounds for a public purpose, which would certainly be worth at least ten times that amount in modern terms. Even when he was twenty-nine his social position was sufficiently assured for his fellow townsmen at Huntingdon to choose him as one of their members of parliament.

Cromwell's concern in politics was motivated, then, by a sense of duty and by religious enthusiasm rather than social resentment. Above all, he was critical of the leadership of the Church. William Laud, the inspiration of the High Church party in the reign of King Charles I and from 1633 Archbishop of Canterbury, had at one time been

27

Archdeacon of Huntingdon. One of Laud's closest friends, Matthew Wren, was Bishop of Norwich and afterwards of Ely. In the only speech that Cromwell is known to have delivered in the first parliament of which he was a member, he expressed his indignation about this so-called "Arminian" group in the Church of England who, he thought, were preaching and practising "flat popery". He quoted the evidence of his old schoolmaster, Dr. Beard, in support of allegations against Richard Neile, the Bishop of Winchester, who later became Archbishop of York. Neile, Laud, and Wren were frequently condemned by the Puritans in the House of Commons as being not only ritualists but of unsound opinions, believers not in "election by grace" but in the arch heresy of free will. Thus Cromwell developed into an active and aggressive Puritan. It is true that, apart from his unique speech in 1629 and a letter in which he described his conversion, written in 1638, we have no reliable evidence earlier than 1640 to sustain this view. But from then on the evidence accumulates, showing religion to be his chief concern and that he had become recognized as the spokesman of radical Puritanism in the eastern counties. On that subject he proved himself to be an eloquent and fervent speaker whose warmth and keenness forcibly struck all who met him.

During the twelve years between the date of Cromwell's conversion and the meeting of the Long Parliament in which he first became absorbed into national affairs, the House of Commons met only twice for brief sessions. Cromwell's life until he was over forty was occupied as a farmer and small landlord whose only interests outside his home and family were comparatively small local matters. When he returned home to Huntingdon after attending the exciting session of 1629, for example, he concerned himself with the question of the new borough charter. This charter, granted by King Charles I, substituted a mayor and twelve aldermen appointed for life for two bailiffs and twelve councillors annually elected. Cromwell objected to the manner in which the new town government was using its powers, and delivered what were described as "disgraceful and unseemly speeches." He was asked to appear before the Privy Council and explain himself. He maintained that the burgesses were being abused in their rights in the common land. The Lord Privy Seal thought that Cromwell's complaints were not unjustified and recommended changes in the charter. Cromwell admitted that he had spoken "in heat and passion", and offered his apologies. Another and not dissimilar incident, dating from the time when he moved to Ely, related to a proposal to drain the Fens. He thought that members of the draining company had been given unfair advantages in the distribution of the reclaimed land at the expense of the Ely burgesses. Again the central government was obliged to intervene, and it was laid down that until the drainage was fully completed there should be no infringement of customary rights. Later still, Cromwell acted on behalf of his former neighbours at St. Ives, and argued so vehemently in the commoners' cause in a parliamentary committee that the chairman threatened to report him to the House.

Such was Oliver Cromwell's fiery character before the civil wars. He was a natural leader of men, readily roused to anger by what he thought to be justifiable grievances; he had a vigorous personality and a sharp temper that was quickly roused; and he was a rough-and-ready speaker. Above all, he was a man of generous instincts and social conscience. A curious little note has come down to us from his days in Ely. It was written on behalf of an old invalid named Benson to a collector of revenues for a local charity. It read:

"I desire you to deliver forty shillings of the town money to this bearer, to pay for physic for Benson's cure. If the gentleman will not allow it at the time of the account, keep this note, and I will pay for it out of my own purse."

So life went on in the land during King Charles I's eleven years of personal administration, while Cromwell moved from Huntingdon to St. Ives, and St. Ives to Ely, and acted as a Justice of the Peace and a self-appointed champion of burgesses with a grievance. The principal cause of discontent in the counties was the King's raising of revenue by extraordinary prerogative means instead of by parliamentary grants. But the early sixteen-thirties were a period of peace and relative prosperity in the country. The burdens upon small property owners were not excessive. Though the King's efforts at administrative reform were unsuccessful, at least there was obvious goodwill behind them. Regular parliamentary sessions had not yet become a recognized feature of English political life, and when the House of Commons was not in session at Westminster there was no accepted centre where grievances against the Crown could be focused. Newspapers did not exist and news travelled slowly, coffee-houses were in their infancy, and taverns absorbed in local gossip; while busy farmers rarely had occasion to go to London. It was not until after the King was launched upon two wars against his Scottish subjects, which required the improvised raising of money and soldiers in a cause with which the English Puritans could not sympathize, that deep feelings were stirred and that parliament had to be recalled. The abject failure of the King in these two wars, which undermined his authority and damaged his prestige, was among the proximate causes of the civil wars in England.

Chapter Three

Origins of the Civil War

"THE religion of England", wrote John Evelyn towards the end of the Protectorate, "is preaching and sitting still on Sundays." This was not precisely as it was but much as the Puritans wished it to be. Their drive to simplify church services, to abolish ritual, to ensure austerity upon the Sabbath day, and finally to reduce or destroy the powers of the bishops, was consistently resisted by the monarchy. Aided though she was by such conscientious administrators as Archbishop Whitgift and Bishop Bancroft of London, it was Queen Elizabeth I herself who had been the real obstacle to the progress of the Puritan movement during her reign, even if it had received support from some of her most intimate lay advisers and from within the House of Commons.

When King James I came to London he listened to the claims of the Puritans for reform at a conference held in Hampton Court in 1604. He allowed the Puritans to put their case and examined what they had to say. But they responded in a heavy-handed and tactless way, and turned the King against them. It is possible that for the same reasons as Queen Elizabeth, the new monarch would in any case have rejected much of the Puritan position. But the Puritans certainly believed that, coming as he did from Presbyterian Scotland and reared in the Calvinist doctrines, King James was reasonably friendly towards them. Clearly he was not impressed by the truculence of their chief adversary, Bishop Bancroft. But a born controversialist himself, the King was revolted by the Puritans' arguments, telling them that their aim was to "strip Christ again", and he "peppered them soundly". Although some points were conceded to them, afterwards Convocation passed new canons enforcing conformity, and it has been estimated that about three hundred clergy were suspended or deprived of their functions in consequence.

As his reign went on, King James I grew more emphatically anti-Puritan. In May 1618 he published a "declaration of sports", allowing his people to play games, drink ale, or take part in Morris dances after they had attended service on Sundays. Moreover, the King came to regard the Puritans as subversive elements in much the same way that his predecessor had done. He once said that "his mother and he from their cradles had been haunted with a Puritan devil which he feared would not leave him to his grave; and that he would hazard his crown but he would suppress those malicious spirits". Yet Puritanism was dominant in the House of Commons, and at its very first meeting in his reign defiantly declared that the King could not alter the religious laws of the country without its consent.

King James's Queen was a Roman Catholic (though by birth a Danish Lutheran), and several of his councillors had Roman Catholic affiliations. But the Court was not, in fact, Catholic in tone, and there was no question of the King wishing to come to terms with the Papacy after the discovery of the Gunpowder Plot against him, which had been organized by Roman Catholics. Moreover, the King was a Calvinist in theology. When he sent over representatives to discuss doctrine with the Dutch at the Synod of Dort, he approved an attack upon the "Arminians", who believed in free will as opposed to predestination, though he instructed his delegates to moderate Calvinistic asperities. He appointed George Abbot, who looked favourably upon the Puritans, as Archbishop of Canterbury in succession to Whitgift, preferring him to Lancelot Andrewes, one of the adopted fathers of modern Anglo-Catholicism. King James I was also doubtful about the wisdom of conferring promotion upon William Laud, the outspoken and unremitting antagonist of the Puritans. Thus, while the first Stuart King had scant sympathy with the Puritan approach and disliked their "prattling sermons", their unpremeditated prayers, and their disruptive or subversive tendencies, he was equally opposed to the "Arminians and Papists", and when he died, the Puritans, though still restlessly trying to capture the Church, had not yet been provoked into a revolutionary frame of mind.

Upon King Charles I's accession to the throne the situation changed sharply. The new King had been brought up in the faith of the Anglican Church, was an austere Christian gentleman, unlike his father a lover of order and ritual, with a French Roman Catholic wife. From the outset of his reign he took extremely seriously his duties as Supreme Governor of the Church and Defender of the Faith. He was determined to impose uniformity and decency upon the Church, and he selected William Laud as his principal adviser; Laud was first Bishop of London, reputedly the most Puritan of dioceses. In 1633 King Charles I appointed him Archbishop of Canterbury on Abbot's death, and encouraged him, as Queen Elizabeth I had impelled Archbishop Whitgift, to repress the Puritan movement.

As soon as he became archbishop, Laud revived an old practice of 'visitations' by bishops to ensure religious uniformity. Under his advice the King refused to allow the Puritan lecturers to preach without the approval of the local bishop, even if their services were paid for by laymen. Orders were given that afternoon sermons, the delight of the Puritans, were to be done away with and catechizing to take their place. The authorities made no secret of the fact that they preferred the reading of homilies to the emotional exhortations of Puritan-minded clergy. The communion table, which was often placed in the middle of the nave and only sometimes moved from there for the administration of the sacraments, and in the meantime proved useful as a hatstand or writing desk, was by the archbishop's order to be placed at the east end of the church and treated as an altar; the Book of Sports was re-issued; the ecclesiastical prerogative court of High Commission was vigorously employed to uphold Catholic ritual; offending churchmen were called upon to take an oath before answering questions put to them there. In 1633 the Attorney-General brought an action before the

Court of Exchequer against the Puritan group in London which was buying up impropriations with the object of peopling the Church with its own sort of clergy, and had it suppressed. Parishioners were told to attend their own churches and not to stray elsewhere in search of more popular sermons. Finally, the King openly approved of the so-called English "Arminians", who believed in free will, rejected rigid Calvinism, and favoured the retention of Catholic ceremonies. The King insisted that it was the sole right of himself and the Convocation of his clergy to determine the doctrine and practices of the Church. That was denied by the Commons and by the Puritans in general.

It is not easy to estimate numerically the distribution of the Puritans throughout the country. Many influential people agreed with criticisms of the bishops without necessarily accepting all the Puritan tenets or wishing to transform the Church. The word Puritan, after all, was a catch-phrase or term of abuse and covered a multitude of beliefs and attitudes. There were, besides the Presbyterians of Scottish as well as English hue, various separatists, Brownists (after a certain Robert Browne), Independents, Congregationalists, Baptists, or Anabaptists, Peculiar or other, with a number of leaders and small groupings in different parts of the nation. Thus no statistical guess about the Puritans of the time is satisfactory. Puritanism was powerful in London, the outports, like Hull, and the clothing towns of Yorkshire and Lancashire, and it had a grip upon merchants and industrialists. Churches set up by Protestant refugees from the Continent, largely craftsmen, at places like Norwich and Canterbury, were allies of English Puritanism. It had strong intellectual support in Cambridge University from the time of Queen Elizabeth I, and was popular in the eastern counties, where Cromwell was reared. On the other hand, it hardly touched Wales or the south-west corner of England, and in all likelihood it was weakest in precisely those western areas which proved most loyal to the King in the civil wars.

But Puritanism was unquestionably fully represented in the House of Commons, which was more Puritan than the country. In the third parliament of King Charles I's reign several attacks were launched upon the bishops, in which Cromwell took part. Sir John Eliot, himself no Puritan, asserted that the bishops could not be trusted with the interpretation of the Thirty-nine Articles. John Pym claimed it was the duty of parliament to stamp out "Arminianism". Already Puritan ministers were seeking refuge in Holland and in New England and Puritan congregations were beginning to emigrate. The King actually considered prohibiting sailings.

The Puritan leaders were neither poor enthusiasts nor obscure fanatics. Robert Rich, Earl of Warwick, and Robert Devereux, Earl of Essex, were Puritan sympathizers among the aristocracy, and they acted in association with men like John Hampden, a wealthy Buckinghamshire landowner, John Pym, a West Country squire of great business ability, and successful barristers like Oliver St. John and William Lenthall. This group was concerned to establish a Puritan settlement in a small island off Nicaragua, whence piratical attacks upon the Spanish "papists" might be initiated. Their plan failed, and other Puritans tried to form a colony in Connecticut. These commercial enterprises afforded the opportunity to create the nucleus of a Puritan opposition to the royal supremacy.

But the early opposition among the gentry to the policy of the Crown in the reign of King Charles I was less of a religious than a constitutional character. "Gentlemen," observed John Selden, "have ever been more temperate in their religion than the common people, as having more reason, the others running in a hurry." Towards the end of the previous reign King James I had reluctantly involved the nation in a war with Spain, under the influence of his favourite, the first Duke of Buckingham, who had also become the personal friend of the heir to the throne. To pay for the war, King James I, like Queen Elizabeth I, had been compelled to alienate Crown lands, and his financial advisers had sought desperately for expedients to refurbish his coffers. Proposals for abandoning outmoded feudal dues in return for a subsidy to be voted by the Commons had broken down. Then the King had exacted "impositions" over and above the usual customs dues in the nominal cause of regulating trade by right of his prerogative. It was because they disliked such methods of raising money, as well as the foreign policy of Buckingham, that the first House of Commons in the reign of King Charles I had refused to grant the King the right throughout the reign to levy customs duties, known as "tonnage and poundage". Thus from the outset the new King was in grave difficulties.

The second parliament of the reign equally refused to vote taxes until the grievances of the nation had been redressed. The monarch then sent a demand through the Justices of the Peace for a "free gift", and when the response was poor, turned to a "forced loan" to secure the amount that had been denied to him by parliament. Several leading parliamentarians, including Sir John Eliot, John Hampden, and Sir Thomas Wentworth, refused to pay, and seventy-six recalcitrants were sent to prison. A test case upheld the King's right to commit his subjects to prison without "cause shown". Although a largish sum was produced by such methods, the King's government still could not meet the costs of the unsuccessful war being waged against Spain. Soldiers were billeted to the displeasure of unwilling hosts at various homes throughout the country, and in 1628 a general election was held to which such "martyrs of the loans" who stood were all returned. In this parliament Oliver Cromwell represented the borough of Huntingdon. Whether he was a "martyr of the loan" or not is uncertain, but he was a cousin of one of them, John Hampden; he now found himself the member of a parliament seething with indignation against the government's policies. It was led by the most celebrated figures of his time—Eliot, Wentworth, Pym, Digges, and the aged Sir Edward Coke—all of them eager to launch a formidable assault upon the government of which the Duke of Buckingham was the leading spirit and all claiming vehemently that forced loans and imprisonments without cause shown were contrary to the fundamental laws of the kingdom.

The parliamentary leaders of King Charles I's and

King James I's reigns were steeped in a constitutional approach which was dependent upon a profoundly false view of history. Most of the landed gentry who filled the House of Commons had received their higher education at the Inns of Court, which have been described as the third university of the time, while other members were professional barristers. All of them had thus acquired the idea that the monarchy was, and always had been, subject to "fundamental laws", those laws being comprised of what was called the law of nature, or the law of reason, the moral law, or the laws of God, and above all the Common Law, or case law, dating back to time immemorial. The high priest of the Common Law was Sir Edward Coke who, though a servant of the prerogative under Queen Elizabeth I, has earned the modern title of the "father of the Whig interpretation of history". Coke thought that the rule of law and the jury system both dated back to before the Norman Conquest, and that the Common Law, representing, as it did, the wisdom and experience of all the subsequent ages, was infinitely superior to the reason of any mere man. The Common Law, in his view, was expressly designed by Providence to preserve the English Commonwealth against arbitrary government. Magna Carta was to him the historical reaffirmation of pre-Norman law, while the House of Commons itself he believed to have originated at least in the time of King Henry I, if not in that of Edward the Confessor. Such persuasive myths were used with gusto to support the attacks made by Coke and his disciples on King Charles I's arbitrary taxation and the imprisonment of members of parliament.

The monarchy, for its part, forced upon the defensive by its growing financial needs, extended practices which had been employed by the Tudors in order to achieve independence from an increasingly assertive House of Commons. After all, had not Queen Elizabeth I exacted "ship money" by prerogative and arrested her subjects, including M.P.s, without cause shown? Admittedly, the advisers of the early Stuarts pressed the prerogative powers pretty hard. But both historically and practically there was no question that the executive could take such action as it thought fit during what it regarded as a national emergency in the interests of the general good of the country. The two early Stuart kings were reasonably suspicious of the historical interpretations of the rights of the courts and of parliament as presented by constitutional lawyers and antiquarians. The Society of Antiquaries, to which scholars like Sir Robert Cotton and Sir Henry Spelman (both famous figures in the historiography of Great Britain) belonged, antagonized King James I, and King Charles I tried to impound Coke's papers after he died. Magna Carta, as well as the Petition of Right, was invoked to condemn King Charles I's treatment of the "martyrs of the loan". Clause 39 of Magna Carta was quoted with enthusiasm, and the King had been obliged to agree that he was bound by this ancient document. Yet history was broadly upon the side of the King.

The trouble was that King Charles I had allowed his prerogative rights to be stretched and stressed to an offensive extent, partly in an understandable reaction against the growing claims to political power, which, under the guise of dubious precedents, were being increasingly put forward by the Commons. While one ought not to place too much emphasis on all this in assessing the origins of the civil war, it is important to remember that the appeals that were made by critics of the monarchy for the purification of the ancient constitution, like the Puritans' pleas for the purification of the Church, were a dressing up of a revolutionary outlook in a pseudo-historical garb. The King wanted to attain financial independence for the Crown and impose uniformity upon the Church, and the means by which he attempted to do so were perfectly in accordance with the practices of earlier English monarchs.

But though the leadership of parliament was thus, in fact, revolutionary, no small group of fanatical plotters can be named who conspired to bring a revolution about, such as may be detected in revolutions in our own times : John Pym was no Lenin or Hitler or Mao Tse-tung. The constitutional assault upon the monarchy, which was primarily inspired by the dislike of the Duke of Bucking-

ham's policies and administration, found its open justification in the Petition of Right and later in the Grand
Remonstrance, and the Acts passed in the first year of the
Long Parliament were a general expression of opinion
within the House of Commons and not of any "formed
opposition" in a later sense. The King had only a handful
of spokesmen or "courtiers" within the House, and men
who later became Royalists were all anxious to reform the
monarchy and the Church. The numerous analyses of the
composition of the House of Commons dividing it into
Court and Country 'parties' or into Parliamentarians
and Royalists do not throw any complete light on the
social impulse behind the civil wars. It was unquestionably the middle classes, including London merchants and
a rising professional group, well represented in the Commons, who gave the impulse to the original attacks upon
the monarchy; whether among these middle classes there
was a driving group of "backwood squires", as one historian asserts, or of politically-frustrated merchants, as
another claims, is a matter for argument; undoubtedly
when it came to the crux, some members of these classes
drew back and found that their traditional loyalty to the
Throne and the Church demanded that they should fight
for the King and not against him. But right up to the
beginning of the first civil war, apart from a few officials,
the whole of the House of Commons—that essentially
middle-class institution—was in broad agreement that the
prerogative powers of the monarchy must be restricted,
and hoped to come to a settlement of the kingdom upon
that basis.

Oliver Cromwell once said that it was not religion that
originally brought about the civil wars, but that it came to
that in the end by way of "redundancy". Up to 1638 when
Charles I tried to impose a version of the English Book of
Common Prayer by force upon Scotland, the main
grievances and ambitions of the parliamentary class
against the Crown were of a political nature, relating to
financial exactions, such as forced loans, impositions,
monopolies, ship money, revived feudal dues, billeting and
requisitioning, and the means by which they were ob-

tained. Thus the whole question of the prerogative powers
was raised and re-examined in the light of the so-called
"fundamental laws" of the kingdom. But parallel to this
was the Puritan rejection of ritualism and ecclesiastical
uniformity as pursued by Archbishop Laud fully backed by
King Charles. Puritanism lent inspiration to many of the
parliamentarians: "The preachers," Professor Haller has
said, "were the men who did most in the long run to prepare
the temper of the Long Parliament." It was Puritanism that
aroused, by its spiritual or ideological appeal, the ardour of
Oliver Cromwell, and men like him who in the last resort
were prepared to do battle with the monarchy; and it may
be doubted if without that inspiration the parliamentary
armies would have had the moral strength to overcome the
disappointments and setbacks of the first year of the war.
Indeed, one Puritan wrote at the time : "Kings and armies
and parliaments might have been quiet this day if they
would have let Israel alone." As Dr. C. V. Wedgwood has
said, when the war came there was a wonderful ferment, a
sort of cracking of the surface, which clearly derived from
the individualistic approach of Puritan Christianity; and
when victory was finally won it was naturally the extreme
Puritans rather than the moderates who acquired the
power in the land. To that extent it is fair enough to
describe the overthrow of the monarchy and the Church in
the middle of the seventeenth century as a "puritan"
revolution. But the origins of the movement against the
monarchy were to be sought in the expansion of a politic-
ally-conscious middle class, which had enhanced the
assertiveness of the House of Commons, armed with the
increasingly significant power of the purse, ever since the
early years of Queen Elizabeth I's reign.

Chapter Four

The Outbreak of Civil War

CHARLES I was "a small fastidious king". In his youth he was described by the Venetian envoy as "very grave and polite" and "with no other aim but to second his father". His elder brother, who died young, was by all accounts an attractive boy, and Prince Charles was overshadowed by him and by the quick intellect of his father. That may explain his stutter, which he never overcame. At first his relationship with his father's favourite, the Duke of Buckingham, was ambivalent; but he lost his jealousy, and a friendship was cemented between them when they travelled together to Spain in search of a royal bride. On the first night of the new reign, Buckingham lay in the King's chamber. Three years later he was stabbed to death in Portsmouth. King Charles never forgave either the House of Commons or the Puritans for Buckingham's assassination which, though carried out by a fanatic with a grievance, was influenced by the vehemence of the political accusations spread against him.

In the King's nature was a streak of obstinacy. He said that he could not defend a bad nor yield in a good cause. Though he loved his wife, who was a stronger character than he was, he did not much care for statesmen of spirit, and did not send for his ablest minister, the former parliamentary leader, Thomas Wentworth, whom he had created Earl of Strafford, until it was too late to prevent disaster to his throne. Later he mishandled his nephew, Prince Rupert of the Rhine, the soldier who might have won the civil war for him. He preferred less able advisers, and was never really in touch with the people he ruled, as Queen Elizabeth I had been. He took after his father in his devotion to hunting, although he also had a taste for art and music; but he tended to let affairs of State fall under the control of his less competent servants.

In the parliament of 1628–9 prolonged attacks had been directed against the King's "evil counsellors", and continued even after the Duke of Buckingham was stabbed to death. Eliot, Pym, and a group of nine, who gathered to concert tactics at the Three Cranes tavern in London, claimed that the King had no right to levy taxation without the consent of the House of Commons, and added, somewhat irrelevantly, that to seize the goods of a member of parliament because he refused to pay customs duties was a breach of privilege. They also insisted that it was parliament's right to interpret the doctrines of the Church of England and not that of the Supreme Governor or the clergy in convocation. In the Commons, too, claims were staked to regulate trade and prescribe foreign policy. While the lawyers and antiquarians in this parliament found plenty of ingenious precedents for such demands, in terms of history they were in reality far-reaching and revolutionary. Everything was wrapped up in becoming language : classical authors were quoted, medieval chronicles were invoked, the King was spoken of with extraordinary deference. Yet before the parliament was prorogued by Charles I, the Speaker, the royal representative in the Commons, was pinned down in his chair while the House defiantly resolved that the King's levying of tonnage and poundage was illegal and that anyone who attempted to introduce "Popery or Arminianism" into the State was a capital enemy. This was a direct assault upon the King's policy in Church and State, and Charles I promptly dissolved parliament and ordered the arrest of its leaders who had foregathered at the Three Cranes.

Affronted by the challenges of the Commons to what he regarded as his inherited rights, the King now set out to govern without calling parliaments at all : he concluded peace with France and Spain, raised money by various expedients, leaving most of his debts unpaid, and depended upon the judges (who could be dismissed at his orders) to uphold his actions as being compatible with his prerogative powers. A principal source of royal revenue was "ship money", which was at first levied upon the ports of the country in 1634 in order to pay for the navy, and was fully in accordance with precedent. When the writs for raising ship money were extended from the ports to inland towns a number of gentlemen refused to pay, as they had previously refused to contribute to the forced loans. Cromwell's cousin, John Hampden, was involved in a test case over ship money in which weighty historical and constitutional arguments were deployed on both sides. Although the case was finally decided in favour of the Crown in 1638, a minority of the judges dissented and the arguments brought forward by defending counsel made a profound impression on the educated classes. Afterwards, ship money, which had been universally unpopular, became extremely hard to collect.

About the same time, martyrs were made of three Puritan propagandists, including the antiquarian, William Prynne, while a London apprentice of precocious talent named John Lilburne was whipped and put into the pillory for distributing tracts. This last incident evidently disturbed Oliver Cromwell, for later he angrily attacked the government for its cruelty to Lilburne. The King's foreign policy also failed to commend itself to the Puritans. In 1630 King Charles I concluded a treaty with Spain which allowed Spanish silver to be minted in England, and then transported to Amsterdam to pay the Spanish armies fighting against the Dutch. This indirect assistance to the Spanish empire against fellow Protestants, a startling reversal of Queen Elizabeth's policy, was a source of much Puritan indignation.

But what brought about the end of King Charles I's period of personal rule was neither his financial nor his foreign policy, but the war that he waged against his own subjects, the Scots. The King had neglected Scotland, but in 1638, in pursuance of his desire for religious uniformity, he tried to impose a version of the Book of Common Prayer upon Scotland, where many of the people were convinced Presbyterians. The King soon recognized that this could only be done at the point of the sword. The Scottish Calvinists retorted by organizing a National Covenant by which they swore to defend their severe but beloved religion to the utmost of their power for all the days of their lives. King Charles I, ignoring the restraining advice of the Earl of Strafford, his Lord Deputy in Ireland, and the fact that he possessed no regular army and very little money, rode north in the summer of 1639, bent upon enforcing his will; but when his troops eventually crossed the Tweed they were repulsed by a fanatical Covenanting army, and he was compelled to patch up a temporary and humiliating peace.

The Scottish Assembly of the Kirk then met and abolished the bishops (who had been reintroduced in a modest way by King James I), and made it plain that it intended in future to prescribe the religious policy of his northern kingdom. This striking Scottish example strengthened and stimulated the English Puritans : could not they, too, transform the Church and be rid of the bishops? But the failure of what was called the first bishops' war did more than that. By calling up the nobility to fight at their own expense against the Scots with the aid of an untrained militia, the King angered the wealthy and influential magnates of the realm whom he had already pinpricked with his ship money and other exactions. At the same time he infuriated the inhabitants of the unruly north by billeting his makeshift army upon them and requisitioning supplies for its support. Moreover, the costs of the war put the government in such financial difficulties that no alternative remained open to the King but to recall an English parliament and ask humbly for money.

The House of Commons that assembled in the spring of 1640—to which Oliver Cromwell was elected as one of the two members for Cambridge—was treated by the King as though everything that had happened during the eleven years since the last parliament had met had been perfectly normal and proper, and as if its only duty was to vote him taxes so that he might affirm his authority over his Scottish subjects. Understandably, the new House, which contained many of its old leaders, apart from Sir John Eliot who had died in prison, was unwilling to lay aside its previous complaints about royal policy, particularly those that concerned the privileges of its own members. Inspired by John Pym, a parliamentarian of genius, it turned back the clock, protesting once again against the levying of tonnage and poundage without its consent and the introduction of what it regarded as novelties into the Church by the archbishops or their fellow "Arminians". Pym also called attention to "grievances against the propriety of our goods", including "that unparalleled grievance of ship money", impositions, monopolies, misuse of the prerogative courts, and the revival of medieval methods of raising money. The claim was urged, although seldom in so many words, that parliament had the right to speak "for the nation", and even veiled threats were not wanting. "We know," said Pym, "how unfortunate Henry III and other princes have been, by the occasion of such breaking of their laws"; that is, "the fundamental laws of the realm". Where was the new Simon de Montfort? The death of Sir John Eliot upset the Commons, as the assassination of Buckingham had provoked the King. An attempt, suggested by Strafford, to use the House of Lords and Convocation to counter-balance the Commons merely annoyed its members the more. Possibly a moderate approach by the King with an immediate offer of concessions might have improved the temper of the House, but when the proposal was put forward by his ministers to waive ship money in return for a grant of subsidies, it came too late, and after three weeks the "Short Parliament" was dissolved.

In spite of this distinct rebuff to his plans, the King was determined to renew the war against the Scots, and once more resorted to ship money and forced loans to pay for it. He himself again journeyed north to direct the campaign, and summoned the Earl of Strafford to assist him. The City of London refused to lend money, and riots took place there. Though both Strafford and Laud favoured vigorous action, the outlook was hopeless. The King called up the militia again, this time from points as far distant as Devonshire and Cornwall, thus widening the area of dissatisfaction with the demands of the Crown. The soldiers were the scum of the land, untrained, undisciplined, insufficiently armed, and many deserted. Not only the former leaders of the Commons but also some of the peers turned against the King and appear to have entered into secret communication with the Scottish Covenanters. Another humiliating treaty was concluded at Ripon by which the Scottish army was allowed to remain on English soil (it had crossed into north-east England) until reparations had been paid and a new parliament was called to meet in November 1640. This was the famous "Long Parliament" in which Cromwell was again elected a member for Cambridge.

The structure of the Long Parliament has been closely analysed by modern historians, but we do not know a great deal about the elections. Broadly it seems to be true that "the richest and most populous part of the country (with the exception of Somerset) declared against the King" and that relatively few "courtiers" were chosen. Pym is supposed to have ridden about the country "to promote elections of the Puritanical brethren to serve in Parliament", but there is no proof of any highly organized electioneering.

In this parliament, Oliver Cromwell gradually took his place as an active political leader. He was forty-one, a man of property in Ely, a figure of importance in Cambridge, and a spokesman for the Puritans in the eastern part of England. He was the father of seven children (his eldest son, Robert, had died in 1639), and had been prominent in local affairs at Ely and made many friends in Cambridge. If we may judge from the reports of the debates that have come down to us, his chief concern was over religion. He wanted the bishops to be abolished, as in Scotland, or at least to have their civil powers and political rights taken away from them. He was also anxious that the prayer book should be revised or done away with, that all remnants of Roman Catholic ritual in services should be suppressed, and that more sermons should be preached in every parish. In fact, he was a violent Puritan at this stage in his career. He was a rough but eloquent speaker and an incessant worker upon committees. How was it that this comparatively modest Cambridgeshire gentleman, who took little part in previous parliaments, became by the time the civil war began, a recognized revolutionary leader? Is there any parallel that may be drawn between him and, say, Robespierre in the French Revolution, or Lenin and Mao Tse-tung in the revolutions of modern times?

In the case of these other protagonists of revolution they had devoted themselves through much of their early life to plotting for an ideological cause and to awaiting the great day. But it is impossible to detect in what little we know of Cromwell's first forty years of life any such purposeful devotion. Although he was loosely linked with the group that concerned itself with colonization and evangelization and which staged protests against the King's use of his prerogative, he does not seem to have taken any active part in their early consultations. But one thing may be said : he had for a long time been a convinced Puritan. Neither Eliot nor Pym nor Hampden was a Puritan in the same extreme radical sense that Cromwell was. In his determination to destroy or "make over" (to use a telling American phrase) the Church of King Charles I's and William Laud's ideals and to free it from the tyranny of the bishops, he was dedicated, uncompromising, and single-minded. Like Abraham Lincoln, to whom he may perhaps be best compared as a leader in a revolutionary time, he was a fatalist. He did not want civil war, let alone the destruction of the monarchy. But he was resolved, as it was expressed in a "protestation" signed by him in May 1641, to defend with his life, power, and estate "the true reformed Protestant religion" as against "popery and popish innovations", and to maintain the power and privileges of parliaments, as well as the rights and liberties of the subject, against any form of arbitrary government. If he was obliged to do so, he would raise an evangelist's sword. He, more than any man, gave the revolution its Puritan colouring.

During the first session of the Long Parliament, the Commons conducted an all-out attack upon the King's policies and sought to strip him of many of his traditional powers. English kings had often been attacked before, from Henry III to Richard III, but by their peers. This, however, was essentially a revolt of the gentry, a bourgeois but

hardly an intellectuals' revolution. When the Commons
first assembled the King once again, this time in person,
pleaded for a vote of money to pay for his campaigns
against the Scots. But John Pym, the little bearded orator,
who had already assumed the effective leadership of the
House in the Short Parliament, was now minded, under
cover of old-fashioned phrases about grievances, evil counsellors, and fundamental rights, to create a new constitution in State and Church. Pym was neither the head of a
formed opposition nor even of a country party; with the
exception of a few courtiers, most of whom were spineless,
the whole House was behind him in his offensive upon
"arbitrary government". So also, if it is fair to judge from
the petitions that reached parliament, was a substantial
part of the country. Edward Hyde, who afterwards
became King Charles II's first minister, led an assault
upon the prerogative courts; Sir John Culpepper, later a
keen Royalist, denounced ship money; Sir George Digby,
who within a year was to engage in an army plot on the
King's behalf, proposed a "grand remonstrance" against
the government's iniquities; Sir Edward Dering, another
later Royalist, criticized the temporal powers of the
bishops; Lord Falkland, who died fighting for the King,
exposed what he regarded as the subservience of the judi-
ciary. Thus Pym commanded a formidable all-round or, if
you like, non-party team which rejoiced in the backing of
the Scots. Cromwell was one of his lieutenants.

Pym began by concentrating his fire upon the Earl of
Strafford, the Lord Deputy of Ireland, outstandingly the
most capable of the King's ministers and the greatest
parliamentarian among them. As Strafford was about to
take his seat in the House of Lords, Pym unleashed an im-
peachment against him; that is to say, he caused the
Commons to accuse him of high treason before his peers in
the House of Lords. Strafford hoped and believed that he
could refute every accusation, and by allowing the attack
to fall upon himself alone to relieve the menaces to his
master. Pym was resolved to avoid all miscalculations; even
as he marshalled the charges against the earl, he prepared
a Bill of Attainder, last used in the reign of Queen Mary I,

which would, if passed by both Houses and assented to by the King, warrant the execution of the Lord Deputy upon general grounds without any legal proof of his guilt. The Earl of Strafford put up such a magnificent defence of his actions before the House of Lords that Pym was compelled to make use of this terrible instrument in the end. Strafford, consistent with his heroic determination to save the throne at all hazards to himself, advised the King to consent to his attainder. Reluctantly and weakly Charles I agreed. In our own times, other public men, tortured by dreadful pressures, have also betrayed their beliefs and their friends. It is impossible for any outsider to measure such pressures. But King Charles never forgave himself.

The King had already yielded upon a number of points. Once Strafford was executed in April 1641, he gave way all along the line. The prerogative courts were swept away; ship money and other exactions were declared illegal; other ministers and judges were impeached or frightened into exile; a Bill was passed ensuring that parliament should in future be called at least once every three years. Finally, the existing parliament was permitted to continue sitting as long as it wished to do so.

In so far as the King had any programme of his own at this period, it was to play for time while exploring more desperate plans. He could see that Pym was holding together a loose coalition, and he thought he might in the long run secure help against his unruly English subjects from abroad or even, once peace had been patched up, from his Scottish subjects. The King was invariably optimistic and a tireless weaver of schemes. His Queen, indifferent to the fate of the martyred Strafford and looking at the situation through her French eyes, aspired to organize some kind of military *coup d'état*. But her husband, though he had his political principles—he declared later that he would never betray the Church or his friends (in fact, he betrayed both)—vacillated. He abandoned both Strafford and Archbishop Laud, who, like Strafford, was executed solely for his loyalty to the throne. It was no wonder that Laud recorded in his diary written in prison

49

that King Charles I "knew not how to be or be made great".

In this first session of the Long Parliament, Oliver Cromwell, though extremely energetic in committee and debate, was most insistent upon the need to overhaul the Church. He had moved the second reading of a Bill for holding annual parliaments, which was afterwards converted into the Triennial Act. But he seems to have taken no part in the attacks on Strafford. He wanted to abolish the bishops, and supported what was known as the "root-and-branch" Bill with that end. Pym, however, recognized that at this stage at any rate a far-reaching Puritan policy would confuse and divide his supporters; men like Hyde, Culpepper, and Falkland, though willing to reduce the temporal powers of the bishops, were no more anxious to overthrow the existing Church than they were to destroy the monarchy. Their aim was reform and not revolution. Thus religion was to some extent soft-pedalled while the other pillars of the old Tudor monarchy were toppling. Some concessions were granted to the Puritan point of view, but in 1640 and 1641 Cromwell, because of his eagerness for the destruction of the Church establishment, was regarded as an extremist, and was evidently distressed that the other parliamentary leaders were less enthusiastic for immediate and radical religious changes than he was himself.

The second session of the Long Parliament marked the turning point towards civil war. In his heart King Charles I had never accepted the restrictions that had been forced upon him, and during the later summer he visited his Scottish kingdom in the hope of enlisting allies. He assented to all that was asked of him by the Scottish parliament, and even tried to ingratiate himself with the Covenanters by attending Presbyterian services. Meanwhile in England the cracks were showing in Pym's coalition; not only were old differences over religious questions becoming accentuated, but difficulties arose with the House of Lords which did not care for being dictated to by the House of Commons. To maintain his position, Pym took up George Digby's suggestion for framing a "grand remonstrance", outlining every public grievance ventilated during the reign. At the same time, events in Ireland were coming to the aid of the Puritans. For the Irish Catholics in Ulster rose in 1641 against their alien masters, as the direct result of the withdrawal of Strafford's strong hand. The Irish rebels claimed to be fighting, among other things, for the preservation of the Roman Catholic religion, and the priests were among their ringleaders. Thus a gigantic "Popish Plot", long forecast by the English Puritans, of which the abortive Gunpowder Plot of King James I's was the forerunner, suddenly became a frightening reality. In London they asked might it not happen here?

The Commons, distrusting King Charles I and suspicious of his doings in Scotland (where they had sent a commission to watch him), were unwilling to put an army under his command to suppress the Irish rebellion lest he should turn it, as they believed Strafford had advised him against themselves. When the King returned to London he was presented, not with a firm offer of military aid, but with the Grand Remonstrance. This contained a demand that in future all officers and ministers of State should be appointed only with the approval of parliament. The Remonstrance passed the Commons by a small majority on 23 November.

Oliver Cromwell was enthusiastically in favour of the Grand Remonstrance. The supporters of the King, including Lord Falkland, had tried to postpone or adjourn the debate upon it. According to Edward Hyde, who led the opposition to the Remonstrance : "Cromwell [who at that time was little taken notice of] . . . asked the Lord Falkland 'why he would put it off, for that day would quickly have determined it'. He answered : 'There would not have been time enough, for it would have taken some debate.' Cromwell replied, 'A very sorry one', supposing few would oppose it." Thus Cromwell was astonished by the turn of events and by the deep division in the Commons. After the debate ended, Falkland twitted Cromwell for his bad judgment. Cromwell replied that "he would take his word another time", and then whispered in his ear "that if the Remonstrance had been rejected, he would have sold all he had and never have seen England more". This conversation recalls clearly Cromwell's political excitement and anger with the policies of King Charles I. It also provides some confirmation for another story that Cromwell about that time thought of emigrating to America.

The King, convinced by the narrow vote on the Grand Remonstrance that he had won a large body of friends in the House of Commons, now at last undertook the *coup d'état* for which his Queen had long pressed him. He tried to arrest John Pym and four leading members of parliament with the intention of impeaching them for treason. But the members were warned and escaped to hiding in the city. The city refused to surrender them, and the King, who had no army, realized he was beaten.

By the failure of his *coup* King Charles I played into the hands of his opponents in the Commons, whose leadership naturally passed to the extremists. The shadow of civil war hung over the land, and Oliver Cromwell moved that the kingdom should be put into "a posture of defence"— against the King! A Bill was at last passed for excluding the bishops from the House of Lords, and the two Houses jointly sought the right to control the militia. But during the early months of 1642 both sides still hoped for a compromise over their differences. Although the King, after he had failed to arrest the five members, left his capital and refused to return, he assented to the Bishops' Exclusion Bill and to a plan for selling forfeited Irish land to pay for the suppression of the rebels. He temporized over the command of the militia, but refused utterly to surrender the "power of the sword". While he was once more playing for time, the Queen sailed to Holland to pawn the royal jewels and raise sinews of war, and in April the King vainly tried to gain control of the city of Hull so as to keep open his communications with the Continent and have its arsenal at his disposal. Gradually members of both Houses who sympathized with the King melted away to the north. Pym framed "Nineteen Propositions" requiring for those who remained the complete control of the army and navy as well as of ecclesiastical policy and the right to appoint all ministers of State and judges. This was an ultimatum which the King dared not accept without completely abandoning his own cause. There had been a peace party in his camp, led by Edward Hyde, who had vainly fought the Grand Remonstrance, but the Queen complained even when the King offered concessions over the militia that he was beginning his " old game of yielding everything ". He liked manœuvring; she wanted to fight it out; and after the rejection of the Nineteen Propositions both Parliamentarians and Royalists prepared for war.

In the last resort the civil war came simply because neither side was prepared to trust the other. On the face of it the King had certainly surrendered a good deal, but especially after the attempt to arrest the five members, Pym, Cromwell, and their friends were willing to concede nothing; even the most moderate of the growing party of the King recognized that compromise had become impossible. In the Commons, the extreme Puritans, including Cromwell—the "root-and-branch" men as they were called—took over command. They were the men who had been aroused by the Grand Remonstrance, who thought the bishops had betrayed the Church and were almost indistinguishable from the Irish papist rebels, and who therefore wanted absolute parliamentary control of the militia and of any force sent to Ireland. Throughout the summer small skirmishes took place in different parts of the country, preliminary to the war all saw was coming once the harvest was in.

As in most revolutions, the leadership was in the end grasped by the extremists and the moderates swept aside. On the parliamentary side John Pym, who for all his conservative phraseology had blazed the trail, remained the master mind; on the King's side his determined French Queen. In the autumn of 1641 after the men of the middle had broken away, Cromwell was left revealed as one of Pym's chief supporters, the root-and-branch man *par excellence*.

Yet neither Cromwell nor Pym would have admitted for one moment that they were revolutionaries. They had persuaded themselves that they were defending old in-

stitutions like the Common Law and the Elizabethan
Church against the King's wicked advisers and popish-
minded clergy. Though in fact they were stating in drastic
terms the claims of an expanding middle class to political
power, sustained and inspired by the austerities of their
predestinarian faith, they maintained passionately that
they were acting in defence of an ancient order of English
society. For a purified monarchy and a purified Church
they contended, in the name of parliament and people,
against an arbitrary King. Such at least is what Oliver
Cromwell believed.

Chapter Five

The First Civil War

IT is one of the curiosities of history that both sides in the English civil war asserted that they were fighting in defence of the law and against arbitrary government. For the King could justifiably argue that parliament in 1642 had become arbitrary. Though many of its members had left it, it passed far-reaching ordinances, for which it claimed, with little or no justification, the full force of law : it snatched the control of the militia from the Crown; it soon began to levy taxes without royal assent. In its Nineteen Propositions it had invited the monarchy to deprive itself of practically all its traditional rights. Pointing to the many loyal subjects who had come to join him in the north of England in the summer of 1642, King Charles I was able to maintain that parliament by no means represented the nation, and that he himself stood out as the champion of the silent masses.

Was it, then, a class war? Most historians tell us that it was not, and certainly it is true that among those who took part in it were families divided against themselves: brothers or cousins fought upon opposite sides; the magnates in a number of counties contended against each other. An analysis of the membership of the Long Parliament shows, as Dr. Tawney recently pointed out, that "the two parties appear . . . to be economically and socially much of a piece". The only difference indicated by the statistics of membership is that those who became Royalists were on the average younger than those who supported parliament in the war. An American historian, Professor Paul Hardacre, has written : "The diversity of elements which went to form his [King Charles I's] party precludes pointing to any single touchstone by which the

Royalist can be recognized. No one creed, no one incentive, led men to identify themselves with the royal interest. Antiquity of family could not be relied on; indeed, as far as the lords were concerned, Charles drew his main backing from the families ennobled by James and himself, the members of families elevated to the peerage before 1603 being about evenly divided."

On the other hand, as Dr. Tawney has also observed, membership of the Long Parliament was not necessarily a mirror of the country, and one cannot ignore the evidence of intelligent men like Edward Hyde and the Reverend Richard Baxter, who were alive at the time, that certain sections of the community, notably the "yeomanry" and the weavers, were pretty solidly opposed to the King. Many other testimonies can be brought together to sustain the view that on the one side a large part of the nobility and wealthier landowners were Cavaliers, while many merchants and citizens in the ports and boroughs (where grievances over the King's "arbitrary taxation"—especially ship money and impositions—had sunk deep) favoured the parliamentary cause when the war began. London came to support parliament, and its well-trained militia formed the nucleus of the parliamentary armies. The navy, recruited in the ports, opted for parliament, and the only one of the bigger ports not under immediate parliamentary control, Portsmouth, surrendered at an early stage of the war. Parliament, by its influence over the City of London and the outports of the kingdom—the true centres of business whose temper was, on the whole, Puritan—therefore had the larger financial resources; while the Queen only succeeded with difficulty in buying one shipload of arms from abroad. Although the measure of support made available for King and parliament varied from county to county, a survey of the social outlook at the beginning of the civil war does not conflict with the opinion that the motive force of the revolution was the desire of an expanding middle class for greater political power or that the Puritan attitude to religion furnished its inspiration.

The King hoped to enlist in his cause the traditional

jealousy of the north of England for the more prosperous south, and that was why he first went to Hull and then to York in search of assistance. But his main strength was found in the western midlands and the west of England, though Yorkshire, under the leadership of the rich and influential Earl of Newcastle, was largely Royalist until 1644. From the beginning the King had a recognizable strategy, which was to rally his supporters in the north, the west, and the south-west, keeping open such communications as he could with the Continent from which he hoped to draw arms, and direct a converging threat upon London once the parliamentary armies weakened or grew tired.

The parliamentary leaders certainly had no clearly worked out military plan. John Pym, an astute political strategist, was no organizer of victory like Carnot in the French revolutionary wars, and seems to have depended upon the third Earl of Essex, his commander-in-chief, for all operational decisions. Essex, a melancholy man, was no enthusiast. Like most of the peerage, whose own order was bound up with the monarchy, he did not wish to humiliate the King or compel him to surrender upon the field of battle. It was not until Pym was dead and the powers of the Earl of Essex reduced that the tide turned for the parliamentary side.

The first big battle of the civil war was fought at Edgehill in the midlands on 23 October, 1642, and Essex, who had suffered himself to be strategically surprised before the action, afterwards withdrew on London, allowing the King to occupy Banbury and Oxford. Within three weeks, Prince Rupert, the King's bold young nephew, was menacing the capital at Turnham Green. But the parliamentary command, directed by a Committee of Safety, threw all its resources into a desperate defence of London, and the Royalist army recoiled. The failure of the King to win a decisive victory in the autumn of 1642 proved fatal to him, for time and money were on the side of his enemies.

The King had first hoisted his standard at Nottingham on 22 August. Even before that, Oliver Cromwell had been assigned to military duties. He had been sent into his own constituency of Cambridge to seize the arsenal in the castle and to prevent college plate from being dispatched by Royalist sympathizers to the King. Not only was he successful in this, but he helped to place the whole of Cambridgeshire at parliament's disposal. At the same time he formed a troop of cavalry, with his brother-in-law, John Desborough, as its quartermaster. After his troop had been blooded at Edgehill, it returned to the eastern counties to become the nucleus of a cavalry regiment. Cromwell thus became a colonel in January 1643. He was appointed a member both of the Eastern and Midland Associations of counties organized for war purposes : the former including Cambridge, the latter his birthplace of Huntingdon. By the early spring he was energetically collecting men, money and weapons, including cannon, at Cambridge. His soldiers were largely freeholders or "yeomen", and he laid stress upon the need to have religious men or "men of a spirit" under his command. He later became known as "Old Ironsides" (Prince Rupert is said to have invented the nickname), and his regiment as the Ironside Regiment.

Though Cromwell was over forty when the first civil war began, it was the call of military duty that gave him his chance first to reveal fully to his fellow countrymen the dynamism of his character. War enabled him to exert his power to command in a way that had never been open to him in peace. "You see . . . how sadly your affairs stand," he was writing to the commissioners in Cambridge less than a year after he had raised his first troop. "It's no longer disputing, but out instantly all you can. Raise all your bands : send them to Huntingdon; get up what volunteers you can; hasten your horses." Here is the accent of the future successful general, who knew exactly what he wanted done.

In battling for money and supplies his enthusiasm must have been infectious. "Lay not too much upon the back of a poor gentleman, who desires, without much noise, to lay down his life, and bleed the last drop to serve the cause and you. I ask not your money for myself . . . I desire to deny myself; but others will not be satisfied; I beseech you hasten supplies." That is another letter with an authentic note of urgency written at the beginning of the same summer. "He wept," it was reported on another occasion, "when he came to Boston and found no moneys. . . ." His authority was sustained by passion.

He had an assurance in himself that derived from his Puritan faith· "He seldom fights," noted one of the chaplains, "without some text of Scripture to support him." He is said to have been found all by himself on the eve of the battle of Marston Moor wrestling in prayer with his Bible in front of him. It was the fusion in him of the practical officer—worrying over his soldiers' pay, organizing their food and transport, always looking for a prompt move to bring him to grips with the enemy—with the inspired Puritan, conscious of the righteousness of his cause and certain that God would win his battles for him, which invoked the trust of his men. But there was little of the remote or frightening commander about him. He had, wrote Richard Baxter, "vivacity, hilarity, alacrity"; both in his official letters and in his written orders he was sharp and to the point. He was, observed the Scotsman, Robert Baillie, "universally loved as religious and stout".

In forming, training, and arming his regiment, Oliver Cromwell was in his natural element. As John Buchan wrote, "This was perhaps the happiest stage of Oliver's life" and he married "the precision of a man of affairs with what he now felt to be a natural genius for war". Though he proved himself to be a superb strategist, notably in the Preston and Worcester campaigns, and was revealed in the battles where he commanded as a tactician of ability, it is right to say that Cromwell's genius as a soldier, as with that of most other great generals, was above all as a trainer and organizer. It is sometimes remarked that in the civil wars, God was upon the side of the big battalions. But it was the quality not the quantity of Cromwell's men that enabled him to win battles against the odds at Preston and Dunbar, and in the opening phases of the war it was his Ironsides who converted the eastern counties into a secure and fortified base, while much of the rest of the country outside London was being won over by the Royalists.

There was a lull during the winter of 1642. Operations usually ceased during the winter because the English roads were so poor that the troops could not move along them when the weather became bad. But in 1642 both sides still had hopes of peace, though terms submitted to the King in Oxford, where he had now taken up his headquarters, were fierce and out of tune with the military facts. Already Sir Ralph Hopton, commanding an army composed chiefly of Cornishmen, was achieving successes for the King in the west of England, while the Earl of Essex, who had occupied Windsor and Reading, confronted the King without daring to attack him. Meanwhile Queen Henrietta Maria had managed to collect her convoy of arms and landed them at the small port of Bridlington on the Yorkshire coast. Here in Yorkshire a polite campaign was being conducted between the Royalist Earl of Newcastle and the Parliamentarian Lord Fairfax, who had found sustenance in the clothing towns of the West Riding, while Hull, still in Parliamentary hands, incommoded the rear of Newcastle's army. Thus the general position was that the Royalists controlled much of the north and west of England (except for Hull, Gloucester, and Bristol), there was stalemate in the Midlands, while the Parliamentarian forces held London and the Home Counties and the east of England. If the Queen could bring her supplies to her husband in Oxford and if the Eastern Association, where Cromwell was, could be neutralized, the Royalists might, in theory at least, be able to carry out a three-pronged movement upon the capital. Such a plan, if it were seriously contemplated, was, however, quite beyond the capacity of the communications and transport system of the time. Still its possibility was enough to alarm Westminster.

During April, Prince Rupert occupied the agreeable village of Birmingham, and retook Lichfield, thereby clearing the way for the Queen's passage south-west from Yorkshire to Oxford. Cromwell had wanted to make a riposte by attacking Newark, a strategic town in Nottinghamshire upon the River Trent, the fall of which would have seriously unsettled the Earl of Newcastle and ruined the Queen's journey. But although he beat a small Royalist contingent at a skirmish in Grantham, the forces in the area were too weak to assault Newark, and the scheme fell through. Meanwhile, Lord Fairfax and his son, Sir Thomas, won a battle at Wakefield, but on 30 June they suffered defeat on Adwalton Moor. On 13 July the King's army in Oxford won a victory at Roundway Down over Sir William Waller, who had been harassing Hopton in the west, and a fortnight later Bristol surrendered to Prince Rupert. Everywhere the parliamentary cause was abashed.

John Pym and his colleagues in London took strong measures to recover the initiative. They opened negotiations for an alliance with the Scottish Covenanters, and they formed a new army in the Eastern Association, under the command of the Earl of Manchester, with the aim of assisting the Fairfaxes in Yorkshire. Cromwell's talents were recognized by his being appointed Governor of the Isle of Ely and one of Manchester's principle lieutenants. Aroused from his habitual cautiousness, the Earl of Essex in September fought a drawn battle with the King's main army at Newbury, and Gloucester, which had long been besieged by the Royalists, was relieved. Nevertheless the King, always an optimist, had enjoyed a good year. Before it was out Pym, scheming to the last, was dead; Cromwell's cousin, John Hampden, was killed in a skirmish, and the Earl of Essex had been irritated to the point of foolishness by the creation of Manchester's army in virtual independence from his own.

It was obvious that new men and a new administration were essential if the King were not speedily to be restored to his old position. Cromwell himself was to be one of the new men. The younger Fairfax and Sir Henry Vane, the Treasurer of the Navy, were others. In February 1644, parliament set up a Committee of Both Kingdoms to run the war in conjunction with their new Scottish allies; Cromwell was appointed a member. A little earlier, he had been promoted lieutenant-general of Manchester's army, which, by dint of determined recruiting, was brought up to a strength of 15,000 men—less than a division in modern terms, but a sizeable force for those less-ferocious times.

Although the pattern of the war had virtually compelled the English Puritans to accept the Scottish Presbyterian alliance, Cromwell felt more than doubtful about its wisdom. For Cromwell never was nor would be a Presbyterian, and he had no wish to substitute a Kirk staffed with elders for the old Church where the bishops ruled. He realized, of course, as King Charles I did later, that the majority of the English Puritans were Presbyterians, but during the years immediately before and after the outbreak of the civil war a large number of Puritan sects had been forming which rejected the view that the Church must be closely ruled by the State. They insisted that individual congregations had the right to choose and pay for their own ministers, and that the congregation should be the real unit in worship. These Christians held a variety of doctrines, and it is not easy, in spite of all the research that has been done in modern times, to sort out their exact relations and policies.

Cromwell himself, for instance, was known as an Independent, but different explanations of the word are given. In a recent book Mr. Yule suggests that the Independents while requiring autonomy for each congregation did not believe in complete separation from the Church, as did the Brownists and Separatists, sects that are often equated with the Independents. All of them at any rate claimed "liberty of conscience". "Separatism", Dr. Haller says, "was the extreme expression of the religious individualism of Puritan faith and doctrine" which levelled all before God. Possibly it is fair to describe Independency as an attitude of mind rather than a doctrine, and as such it appealed powerfully to Cromwell—who is sometimes said to have been a "spiritual anarchist"—and to his mystical friend, Henry Vane. Therefore when negotiations for an agreement or covenant between the English and Scottish governments were under way, Cromwell and Vane exerted all their influence to prevent the imposition of an exclusively Presbyterian Church upon England and to ensure toleration for the sects. They were aware of the dangers of this alliance, while Cromwell himself, convinced of the quality of Manchester's army, which was largely composed of Independents and sectarians, was by no means convinced that so high a price had to be paid for Scottish aid. He believed, in fact, that the English Puritans could compel the King to come to terms with the English parliament without any outside help. The events of 1644 underlined that belief for him.

The Scottish army, over 20,000 strong, after leaving home in deep snow, entered England in January 1644, and King Charles I was at once thrust upon the defensive. But during the year the fortunes of war swayed to and fro. The Scots moved in a leisurely manner, and for a time Newcastle (now a Marquis) was able to hold them up north of Yorkshire. But meanwhile Sir Thomas Fairfax had dashed from Yorkshire into Cheshire and beaten a Royalist force which consisted partly of soldiers landed from Ireland (where King Charles I's Lord Lieutenant had concluded an armistice with the Catholic rebels); soon after Prince Rupert had likewise dashed across England and relieved Newark, which was under siege by the Parliamentarians. In the same month Sir William Waller had defeated his old friend and foe, Hopton, in Hampshire, the Earl of Sussex had advanced upon Oxford, and the Earl of Manchester was preparing to reconquer Lincolnshire. After his return from Cheshire, Sir Thomas Fairfax inflicted a defeat upon the Royalist governor of York at the Battle of Selby. This defeat, as much as the pressure of the Scots, obliged the Marquis of Newcastle to withdraw into Yorkshire and shut himself up in the county town. Thereupon the Scots came south, joined up with the Fairfaxes, and made ready to besiege York. A message was sent to the Earl of Manchester inviting him to come over from Lincolnshire and share in the siege of what was considered to be the capital of the north.

Manchester's army, having stormed Lincoln, arrived to take part in the siege of York on 3 June, after Oliver Cromwell had gone forward with a cavalry screen. York was an excellently fortified city with a strong garrison, and was extremely hard to assault with the weapons of the time. Even though the besieging armies now amounted to some 30,000 men, the Marquis of Newcastle was able to defy them while he appealed to the King for rescue. Prince Rupert was ordered into Lancashire to collect reinforcements and then use every means in his power to save York. When, towards the end of July, the besiegers learned that Prince Rupert was coming, they raised the siege and moved west in a vain attempt to intercept him, and York had been relieved without a shot being fired.

The question now was whether a battle should be fought. Undoubtedly Prince Rupert who, even with the aid of the tired defenders of York, was numerically inferior to his enemies, could have avoided fighting if he wished; but his spirits were high, he believed that his foe was demoralized, and that his King wished him to undertake a battle; and he persuaded the Marquis of Newcastle to go along with him. Thus, after some marching and counter-marching, the two armies confronted one another on Marston Moor, a few miles west of York, on 2 July 1644.

The battle of Marston Moor was a dramatic struggle. On paper, Cromwell's side had all the advantages, superiority of numbers (27,000 against 17,000), higher ground, the initiative, and the opportunity for surprise. But it lacked a co-ordinated command, and the three armies—Manchester's on the left, the Scots in the centre, and Fairfax's on the right—failed to combine. Since, moreover, according to the military practice of the time, infantry was concentrated in the centre with the cavalry on the wings, some troops of Scottish horse were intermingled with the armies on the wings, and had to accept orders from unknown Englishmen. Further, all the three commanding generals, Manchester, the Earl of Leven at the head of the Scots, and Lord Fairfax—made their own dispositions, and when the battle started fought more or less independently. The Royalists, on the other hand, had only one commander in Prince Rupert, and had the advantage of being attacked in their prepared positions behind a ditch defended by cannon.

The battle did not begin until early evening, after the Royalists had given up expectation of being attacked that day. Cromwell was in charge of the cavalry on the left, and after a temporary check overthrew the opposing Royalists. Prince Rupert, discarding the advantage of his unified command, had taken control on this wing and, when he was defeated there, was too late in resuming command to save the day. Yet elsewhere the battle had gone well for his side. In the centre the Scottish infantry had suffered considerable losses, and on the right the Yorkshire cavalry had been repulsed. After his own victory, however, Cromwell rallied his cavalry, and led them across the battlefield to the aid of his right wing. This was the crucial move with the hall-mark of genius upon it. Not only did he reverse the fortunes of the day there, but subsequently he went tirelessly to the help of the infantry, inflicting crippling losses upon Newcastle's stubborn foot soldiers.

Thus the battle was won largely by a comparatively small group of highly trained cavalry—the men Cromwell had raised in the eastern counties. Cromwell's talents shine clearly across the years. For only an officer of extraordinary character could have kept such control over his men and over the battle when all three of his commanding generals had given it up for lost. From that moment Cromwell himself was recognized as an outstanding soldier, an amateur who had made good.

But Marston Moor was not one of the decisive battles of history. For meanwhile the Earl of Essex had abandoned the siege of Oxford and marched away to seek glory in the west of England, only to suffer humiliation at the battle of Lostwithiel, while Sir William Waller, left behind in Oxfordshire, had been defeated by the King three days before the battle of Marston Moor. Nor did the victors of Marston Moor, after they had occupied York, make any concerted attempt to follow up their victory. The Scots marched back to Newcastle; the Fairfaxes to Scarborough; and Manchester to Huntingdon. Cromwell, who still had only a secondary voice in affairs, chafed at the inaction, and did not scruple to criticize his superior officer in private letters. He also quarrelled with one of his fellow officers, a keen Scottish Presbyterian named Major-General Laurence Crawford, who had won the confidence of the Earl of Manchester. Crawford had insisted that junior officers ought to adhere to the Covenant, an insistence singularly out of place in an army largely manned by Independents. Cromwell stoutly objected, and Manchester had to take his two subordinates up to the Committee of Both Kingdoms in London to resolve their differences. The committee told its generals to stop quarrelling and to get on with the war. Eventually Manchester linked up with Sir William Waller, and confronted King Charles I, who had returned in October from his successful excursion into the west, and a battle was fought at Newbury. On the whole, the King had the better of it, and when winter brought the campaigning season to a close, the victory of Marston Moor had been largely nullified.

It was obviously high time that parliament and the Committee of Both Kingdoms, which directed strategy, undertook some serious thinking. Three campaigning seasons had gone by and final victory was not yet in sight. The Scottish army, though it contributed substantially to the victory of Marston Moor, had not compelled the Royalists to sue for peace. Indeed, King Charles I had found a military genius to reinvigorate his cause in Scotland in the Marquis of Montrose, whose astonishing victories with a handful of men had discouraged the Scots in England from moving too far away from their frontier. The King was still unshaken in the whole of the west and in Wales, and his defensive-offensive strategy, based on Oxford, had paid dividends. The Parliamentarians, for their part, since the death of Pym, were divided among themselves. Their principal commanders, the Earl of Essex and the Earl of Manchester, were lethargic by nature and numbed with anxiety to come to terms with the King if they possibly could. Among the Puritans, the Presbyterians and Independents bickered with each other, and the Scottish Commissioners in London were not averse from stirring up trouble between them. Critics outside the House of Commons were saying that its members found lucrative offices for themselves, and were as often as not profiteers from the war.

Cromwell was not only furious with the failure of the high command to follow up the victory in Yorkshire, but was determined to prevent the Scots from fastening their Kirk rule upon England, replacing old priest with new presbyter. In November 1644 he made a speech in the

Lower House, openly condemning the conduct of his commander-in-chief whom he bluntly accused of "backwardness in all action". Manchester naturally tabled counter-charges, and the Presbyterians played with the idea of indicting Cromwell as an "incendiary". In the end, common sense prevailed and, laying aside recriminations, the Commons decided to form a "new model army" and to introduce a "self-denying ordinance", whereby members of both Houses should lay down their posts and commands and leave the waging of the war to non-political soldiers. Who exactly was responsible for planning these far-reaching resolutions is not clear, but unquestionably Cromwell was foremost among those who favoured them. After some months of manœuvring they were accepted by the Lords, and Sir Thomas Fairfax was appointed to organize and command the New Model Army. Essex and Manchester reluctantly resigned their commands, and other generals, including Cromwell and Waller, were required to lay them down after forty days, though they might be recommissioned. On the face of it, Cromwell's military career was over, and he was statesmanlike in his acquiescence. Still, the reputation he had won at Marston Moor and elsewhere was hard to forget, and he may well have felt that unless the war now went astonishingly well, his chance might come again. And so it proved.

Cromwell had nothing to do with the formation of the New Model Army, but since it contained a high proportion of men who had been recruited originally in the Eastern Association, it included many Independents who were of the same frame of mind as himself. While it was forming, Cromwell and Waller, as a last service, led a cavalry expedition to the west of England, and when Cromwell returned he was ordered to do all he could to disorganize any attempt by the King to leave Oxford to join Montrose in Scotland. Cromwell's period of command was extended for the purpose, and at the end of May, after he had successfully carried out his mission, he returned to Cambridgeshire preparatory to relinquishing his commission and retiring into civil life.

The war now suddenly flared up to its climax. The New

Model Army had failed to distinguish itself in an early campaign in the west, but the sack of Leicester by the Royalists after a surprise attack from Oxford, provoked the Parliamentarians, and Fairfax was given a free hand to seek battle. The King, who had havered over his next move, was cornered with his army north of the village of Naseby in Northamptonshire on 14 June 1645. Before the battle, Fairfax had sent for Cromwell, inviting him (with the approval of the House of Commons but not of the Lords) to take the vacant post of lieutenant-general in the New Model Army, which rejoiced at his return.

The battle of Naseby proved to be a conclusive victory for parliament. Fairfax himself originally commanded the cavalry of the Parliamentarian right, and after success had been won there, handed over to Cromwell and went across to rally his infantry in the centre. Cromwell, as at Marston Moor, by keeping his troopers fully in check, was able to come to the aid of the infantry, and Prince Rupert having, as he often did, overrun the field and lost control on the opposite wing, after a three-hour contest, the Royalists gave in, two men out of every three surrendering upon the field of battle. They had been outnumbered, outfought, and demoralized.

In July the Scottish army came as far south as Hereford, and Fairfax, accompanied by Cromwell, moved his army into the west to deal with the only substantial Royalist force left intact. This army was beaten at the battle of Langport on 10 July, and soon afterwards Prince Rupert surrendered Bristol. By the middle of the following year the first civil war was over. The King fled in disguise from Oxford and surrendered to the Scottish army, which was now at Newark, and Oxford capitulated to Fairfax on 24 June 1646. Before that, Cromwell had finally laid down his commission and gone to London to resume his parliamentary duties. Though Fairfax, an exceptionally capable and much-liked commander, had led the way to final victory, even the Scots, who hated him, recognized that Oliver Cromwell was the hero of the war.

During the war not only had Cromwell proved himself to be a leader of men, an incisive administrator, and tactician who thought swiftly upon the field of battle, but he also suddenly showed himself to be a statesman. Nothing reveals his change of character and control over his temper better than the speech he made first advocating the "self-denying ordinance" which, by securing the command of the New Model Army for General Fairfax, helped to bring victory to the Parliamentarians after their many early failures. In that speech Cromwell had said that now was the time to speak or for ever hold the tongue. He urged that the nation had to be saved from "a bleeding, nay almost dying condition", and that all further delays in military action must be avoided lest the country wearied of the war and came to hate the very name of parliament. In asking his fellow members of the House of Commons to forget their squabbles among themselves and to sacrifice their own private interests for the public good, he struck a note of patriotism with words about "true English hearts" and an appeal to love of "our Mother Country". In a later speech he assured the same members that his own soldiers would gladly fight and die in the cause for which they had enlisted. His trust in his men, as in the nation that they were making, was the counterpart of their confidence in him. It was one of the secrets of his strength, and explains why no other officer or statesman was ever able to overthrow him.

Chapter Six

Parliament and the Army

WHEN the first civil war ended, the victorious side scarcely knew what to do, for it was deeply divided, especially over religious questions. The ferment of new ideas which arose when the organization of the old Church was destroyed (a Bill abolishing the bishops and permitting the sale of their properties had finally been passed in 1646) was extending from religion to politics. At Westminster an assembly of divines and learned laymen were sitting, trying to work out a new ecclesiastical constitution; at the same time, hopes were not abandoned of coming to terms with the King, and proposals for what amounted to a confirmation of everything parliament had done since Charles I had left London were sent to him in Newcastle upon Tyne, where he was still a prisoner of the Scottish army. The King replied by asking permission to come to London and debate the matter. He knew enough about what was going on there to realize that, though beaten in the war, he might be able to play off one group of his enemies against another. But the Scots did not wish to be involved and returned home after handing over their monarch to the English parliament.

The House of Commons now consisted mainly of convinced Puritans. After the war was over a number of elections had been held to fill vacancies in the Commons to replace the Royalists who had been "disabled" for fighting for the King. The outcome of these elections made little difference to the complexion of the House. On religious questions the out-and-out Presbyterians were about equal in number to their opponents, who consisted of the Independents and their sympathizers led by Cromwell and Vane, and of the so-called "Erastians", mainly lawyers, who were anti-clerical in spirit and were resolved that on no account should the Presbyterian Church dominate the State, as it did in Scotland. Thus, while the Independents were able, with Erastian support, to demand a measure of religious toleration in the new settlement of the nation and were backed by their influence over the New Model Army, when it came to other questions they carried no such weight in the House of Commons. Here they relied for the exertion of pressure entirely on the wishes and feelings of the soldiers who had won the war—volunteers for the most part, and not mercenaries, among whom radical opinions were rapidly gaining ground.

During the period 1644-5, Oliver Cromwell had been upon very friendly terms with John Lilburne, a keen Puritan fifteen years younger than himself, who prided himself on having been born the son of a gentleman, but who, as the London apprentice of Puritan principles, had received a rough handling by the government of King Charles I during his "eleven years' tyranny". The two men had a good deal in common; both were visionaries, enthusiasts with an individualistic outlook upon life, and were capable of exercising something of a magnetic power over their fellows; both were absorbed in politics, but had been brought into them chiefly by their religious feelings, particularly their disapproval of the Church hierarchy. Cromwell admired Lilburne for his courage, exemplified in the way in which he underwent martyrdom in his youth for his beliefs. Lilburne was grateful to Cromwell for his patronage and for defending him in the Commons. He respected him as a soldier, served under him as a lieutenant-colonel in the Earl of Manchester's army, and was entirely in accord with Cromwell's criticism of the earl for his dilatory conduct after the battle of Marston Moor. But, more consistently than Cromwell, he refused a commission in the New Model Army because he would not accept the Covenant or the Scottish alliance, and he retired to London to devote himself to political pamphleteering. Out of the faith and grievances of this firebrand, what was known as the Leveller movement was born.

Religion was the basis of this trend towards democracy,

for Levelling was chiefly political and not economic in character. The Calvinist organization of the churches, with the congregations taking a big part in their government, helped to establish a pattern for democratic ideas. But there was a curious dualism about it. To be logical, if some were born elected to eternal salvation and others condemned to everlasting damnation, should it not have been the elect, the "chosen people" and not all of the people who were destined to rule upon the earth? This view was, in fact, held by one Puritan sect, that known as the Fifth Monarchy men, who believed that the time was near when Christ was coming back to earth and that His disciples should prepare the way for Him. But other Puritans took the view that there were two "orders" upon earth—the order of Nature, in which men were inevitably corrupt, and the order of Grace or the Elect. The Elect, they thought, were only concerned with religious questions, with preparing themselves, free from political interference for the after-life; while politics belonged purely to the order of Nature. A millennium might be coming soon, but meanwhile in the order of Nature the defeat of the King in the civil war had opened the way for the formation of a new kind of government, the writing of a fresh constitution in which "the people", who had been deprived of their natural rights and liberties since the Norman Conquest, should at last come into their own again.

John Lilburne, like many other self-educated men of his generation, was profoundly influenced by the teachings of Sir Edward Coke. He was convinced that King Charles I had merely followed in the footsteps of his predecessors along paths charted by Norman kings, in robbing his subjects of their historic birth-rights, by ignoring the "laws of nature" and violating his coronation oath. Whether now in 1647 men should return to the golden age of the past and the "fundamental laws" of the kingdom or march forward to a state of perfection in the future brandishing a freshly minted declaration of rights amounted to much the same thing. The Levellers at any rate wanted a clean sweep of the monarchy, the House of Lords and the Church of England, a reconstituted House of Commons meeting annually, a democratization of the electorate, and finally a constitutional guarantee of the liberties of the individual. Lilburne and his friends did not come to all these conclusions at once, but they came to them pretty quickly in the course of the political transformations that followed the first civil war. They were embodied in various documents ranging from the Levellers' "Large Petition" of March 1647 to the "Agreement of the People" presented to the Council of the Army in October of the same year.

The Levellers' teachings appealed to a fairly extensive following. The Puritans, encouraged to read their Bibles for themselves, to despise priestly intervention with God, and to spurn the discipline of the bishops, had learned to believe in the virtues of religious equality; and because they required freedom from rule either of magistrate or priest when they practised their worship they set store also upon religious liberty. The step from religious equality and religious liberty to civic equality and civic liberty was neither long nor difficult. The Levellers also attracted the soldiers for more practical reasons : by claiming that the parliament must not only submit itself to being frequently called and elected and that there were certain rights of man that no parliament might alter, the Levellers were showing the soldiers that even parliament could be and should be subject to a higher law and to the control of the people at large. And had not they, the volunteers of the New Model Army, who had ground the monarchy to defeat, already acted in the name of "the people"? Indeed, were they not the true representatives of the people, at any rate of the "honest people" of the realm? If parliament, which had used their services when it needed them, now tried to disband them upon miserable terms—as it did— and to formulate a new constitution without their consent, had they not the right to express their opinions, even to insist upon their criticisms and their point of view being taken into the fullest account?

Unquestionably during these years 1646 and 1647 a democratic movement unique in the history of England was making swift headway. It centred upon London; here an effort was exerted to end the oligarchic form of government and to transform several of the city guilds. "If an arbitrary government be so destructive in the Commonwealth," wrote a Leveller pamphleteer in 1645, "surely it is equally dangerous to suffer it in the City." Apprentices claimed that as they had risked their lives in the civil war they, too, had a right to be heard in presenting their case against monopolists of economic power. Lilburne said that "a cruel city" where a group of rich men had usurped the privileges of the freeholders might be a worse tyrant than any. In 1646 and 1647 petitions were presented to the City government, seeking a democratic revision of the existing constitution and asserting that the City Fathers, like Charles I, had broken their trust.

While Lilburne and his followers were reaching these radical opinions, the Independents were also coming to have a distinct political outlook of their own. Up to the end of the civil war they had been largely content to remind the Presbyterians that in any constitutional settlement either of State or Church that might be reached, respect for liberty of conscience for all sorts of Christians was essential. But when they discovered that once the war was won the Presbyterians both in parliament and in the City were planning to disband the army, to suppress the sects, and come to an understanding with the King for an exclusive State Church, they grew restive and angry, and demanded a settlement in which both the King and parliament should be compelled to recognize their claims for liberty as Christians and their rights as men. Thus, during 1647 there was a growing conflict among the Presbyterians, Independents, Erastians, and Levellers, with the Royalists watching and secretly rejoicing at the disputes among their enemies.

Matters were brought to a head when in March the Commons voted that the army must either disband or accept service in Ireland under Presbyterian generals, and the New Model Army retorted by petitioning parliament for its arrears of pay and much more generous terms on demobilization. Parliament voted that soldiers who refused to obey them were "public enemies". In May the regiments retorted by electing agents or "agitators" to represent their point of view in the councils of the army. Fearing that they had gone too far, the majority in the Commons then invited Oliver Cromwell and other M.P.s who had influence with the soldiers to try to come to an agreement with the army. This failed. Cromwell, who for many months had hesitated as to his course of action, now threw in his lot with the army against parliament.

Oliver Cromwell's mind always worked slowly and deliberately. His detractors have argued that he interpreted what he himself wanted to do as the Lord's will, claiming, in common with other but less powerful Puritans of his generation, that he had a private line to Heaven. It seems fairer to say that here was a conscientious man who was always reluctant to change his course of conduct until experience and reflection had convinced him—and convinced him completely—that such a change was imperative. He was suspicious of "fleshly reasonings", by which he meant the temptation to allow his own passions and desires to rule him. Up to 1647 he regarded himself simply as a good soldier loyally serving the community and a member of parliament ready to obey the wishes of the majority. He had expected that the complaints of the soldiers would be fairly met. But gradually he lost his confidence in the leaders at Westminster because they were treating ungenerously the men who had won the war for them. He had told Fairfax : "There want not in all places men who have so much malice against the army as besots them." Like other Independents, he was perturbed by the menace to religious liberty from an all-embracing Presbyterianism; he was aware that what he called "the honest party" in the Commons was in a minority. Finally he realized the vast influence that he commanded among the soldiers for good or ill, and that he might surrender it to extremists if he sided with the parliament against the army. Thus, for the sake of order as well as religious liberty, he crossed the Rubicon.

In May 1647, after his patient efforts at conciliation had failed, Cromwell took one of the most critical decisions of his life. He agreed to the dispatch of a certain Cornet George Joyce into the Midlands to see that the arsenal and artillery at Oxford were properly secured, and that there was no danger of the King getting into the hands of the Presbyterian leaders. After he had been surrendered by the Scots, Charles I had been placed in honourable captivity at Holdenby House in Northamptonshire. When Joyce reached there on 2 June, he decided that there was a real danger of a plot to take the King away to London. Therefore, having gathered a force of five hundred soldiers together, he compelled the King to come away with him, trusting to the revolutionary movement in the army to give him the necessary backing, and to Cromwell to uphold his action. Meanwhile, Cromwell himself left London and joined the army at Newmarket. When Fairfax, who had promptly superseded Joyce, asked on whose orders he had acted, Cromwell admitted that he had agreed to his mission, but said that Joyce had taken the initiative in removing the King into the army's power. But he does not appear to have condemned Joyce for what he did. He thereby committed himself to the army as against parliament.

Cromwell's change of front united the army and frightened parliament. Solemn engagements were concluded, a general council was formed in which both the officers and the common soldiers were represented, and the army then began to march towards London in search of a settlement that would provide for "the peace of the kingdom" and the "liberties of the subject". But these high-sounding phrases were not ones on which the army itself had as yet agreed a meaning.

For Cromwell and the leaders of the army were under very heavy fire from their discontented rank-and-file. Even after the eleven principal Presbyterian members of the House of Commons had voluntarily withdrawn in order to facilitate negotiations between parliament and the army, the Agitators—representing the private soldiers —were urging General Fairfax, their commander-in-chief, Cromwell, and his son-in-law, Henry Ireton, that they should enter London, disarm the city militia, and compel the release of the political prisoners there, including the Leveller chief, Lilburne. Cromwell and Ireton, discussing these demands at Reading on 16 July, thought that they had already gone far enough. Though they had sided with the army against parliament (Ireton was also an M.P.), they were still eager for a reconciliation. "We act as if we did intend only to get the power into our own hands," protested Ireton, "to give the kingdom satisfaction is the thing that we desire." Cromwell wanted them to negotiate a general settlement with parliament on the basis of a document known as "The Heads of the Proposals", which Ireton was preparing and embodied the constitutional and political programme of the army leadership. Ireton insisted that "the honest party" in the Commons was gaining strength and should be encouraged, while Cromwell reminded the Agitators that "what we and they gain in a free way, it is better than twice so much in a forced and will be more truly ours and our posterity's". However, events got out of hand. The Presbyterians in London, under pressure from a mob, forced out the Independents, collected a defence force, and defied the New Model Army. Cromwell's plea for reason at Reading was then perforce ignored, while Fairfax had no alternative but to move his army into London to restore order. The Presbyterian leaders again withdrew from Westminster, and Cromwell and Ireton then tried once more to plan a pacification which would embrace the King, the parliament, and all sections of the army, including both the Agitators and the Levellers.

But the Levellers were unwilling to compromise : the fervour of revolution gripped them, the star lighting up a new Jerusalem dazzled their eyes. They wanted to be done with the old monarchy, to dissolve the existing House of Commons, to elect a new one upon a really democratic basis, and to ensure, as they phrased it in their "Agreement of the People", that the power of the new representatives of the nation should be "inferior only to theirs who choose them"; they envisaged a land where religion was free from all secular interference, where men could not be conscripted into the army, where there were no restraints upon trade, and where all the laws were equal and good. Conscious of the need to keep the army together, a General

Council met at Putney, whence the army had withdrawn from London, to try to reconcile the "Agreement of the People" with Ireton's "Heads of the Proposals", which had been modified to make them palatable to King Charles I.

During the late summer of 1647 Cromwell had devoted all his energies to trying to reconcile parliament, the King, the Independents, Presbyterians, Levellers, and army agitators. Consequently his motives were misinterpreted on every side. The Royalists thought that he was frightened lest the King should punish him in the event of a restoration; the Levellers accused him of intriguing with the King against the army and trying by underhand means to overthrow its democratic spokesman, Colonel Thomas Rainsborough. Cromwell, unperturbed, worked in harmony not only with Ireton but with his old civilian friends, Vane and St. John. Knowing the virulence of rumour, he wrote to a fellow officer in Ireland : "Though it may be for the present a cloud may lie over our actions, to them who are not acquainted with the grounds of our transactions, yet we doubt not but God will clear our integrity and innocency from any other ends we may aim at but His glory and the public good."

The day before he wrote that letter (September 13) he had been to see John Lilburne in the Tower of London. Lilburne had tried to persuade him that parliament was worse than the King, but Cromwell had retorted : "The King's reign was a habit of oppression and tyranny" and denied that the "great men" of the army and parliament were obstructing peace. He offered to obtain Lilburne's release if he would promise to restrain himself; Lilburne would give no precise promise, but nevertheless Cromwell said he would try to procure his liberty and to ease the hardship of prisoners in the Tower. Lilburne's case was at once referred to a parliamentary committee, and later Cromwell again approached him to exert his influence to soothe the fears of the rank-and-file of the army. Even though Lilburne uttered wild threats against Cromwell, he was in fact allowed a substantial measure of liberty during the autumn and winter. Cromwell's remarkable and uncharacteristic patience, when provoked by extremists like Lilburne and Rainsborough, was well exemplified at Putney.

Cromwell took the chair at the Putney meetings in October 1647, and there the "Gentlemen Independents" led by Ireton, on one side, and the Agitators and Levellers, whose spokesman was a friend of Lilburne named John Wildman, on the other, argued out their cases in a spirit of acrimony, tempered by texts. The Levellers claimed that they were now entitled to write a new constitution upon a clean slate, and blamed Cromwell and Ireton for having any dealings at all with the captive monarch. The reply was given that the engagements of the army must be honoured, and that it was legitimate to explore all methods of coming to a settlement. Ireton argued against democracy on the ground that if men without property received a vote the result would be anarchy. The Levellers replied by appealing to the "law of nature", asserting in effect, like the French revolutionaries a century and a half later, that men are born free and equal and should now throw off the chains that had bound them since the days of the Norman kings. Cromwell himself, a conservative by instinct but a radical by force of events, pleaded hard and reasonably for a compromise. But the left-wing in the camp was inflexible.

In spite of these sharp differences of outlook it is conceivable that a plan might have been finally agreed among all the spokesmen of the New Model Army and made acceptable to their friends, the "honest party" at Westminster, if more time had been allowed. It must be remembered that all these people used much the same language and looked upon life in much the same sort of way. They were agreed that a new constitution must be framed in which the House of Commons should take the central part; they wanted the monarchy to be reduced to formal functions, if not to be abolished altogether; they were anxious to have a written "Bill of Rights" whereby, as in the American constitution of later days, certain principles of liberty should be made untouchable and unalterable by any government or legislature; above all, they were resolved that the grievances of the armed forces should be met and fair compensation paid for their long services.

Lilburne and Cromwell were, in fact, as has well been said, "united in the strife that divided them". But the strife remained. And it needed an outside stimulus to repair the breach in the army which had revealed itself during the debate in the General Council. The stimulus was provided by the behaviour of the King. In November 1647, breaking his parole, Charles I escaped from custody at Hampton Court Palace and fled to the Isle of Wight. His object was to obtain a freer hand with which to carry on intrigues that he had begun with the Scottish Commissioners in England, who, disappointed with what they had gained from the English parliament after they had fought in England, thought that they might purchase the King's agreement to the supremacy of their Presbyterian Church in both his kingdoms by restoring him to his throne. The King managed to conclude such an agreement in December from his refuge in the Isle of Wight. He promised to establish Presbyterianism in England for three years, to suppress the Independents, and to grant certain privileges to his Scottish subjects, if the Scots would regain for him his rights as a crowned King. The Commissioners returned home with these proposals while the House of Commons voted that they would negotiate with the King no further (the "vote of no addresses"), and the army leaders, including Cromwell, broke off all discussions with him and ordered his closer imprisonment.

For a third time Cromwell had been obliged to change his mind. When he left London to join the army six months earlier he had still hoped to act as a conciliator between all parties and to frame a settlement in which a place would be found for the King. Now, shocked by the King's breach of parole and his dealings with the Scots, which were an open secret, Cromwell resigned himself to setting aside King Charles I. But he had not yet abandoned his belief in monarchy. Indeed, except for a handful of "Commonwealthsmen"—not necessarily Levellers —all the men of importance on the Parliamentarian side at the beginning of 1648 were still monarchists. Cromwell told Colonel Ludlow, one of these early republicans, that he thought the introduction of a republic into England was theoretically possible but not practically feasible. His idea was to put one of the King's sons upon the throne, provided he was willing to consent to the draft constitution being fashioned by Ireton.

At any rate, King Charles I's last bid to regain his throne enabled his enemies to close their ranks. When in the spring the Royalists responded to the signal for a new rising and the Scottish Engagers prepared to invade the north of England, General Fairfax and Lieutenant-General Cromwell marched out to wage the second civil war in the fullest confidence that the bulk of their armies would follow them loyally until victory was won again. The volatile John Lilburne hastened north to offer Cromwell his moral support.

The year 1647 is crucial in Cromwell's biography. His critics then and later accused him of perfidy, of fawning upon the King only to betray him; of making promises to the Levellers which he did not intend to keep; of using the army against parliament; of preparing the way for his own future personal aggrandizement. Few statesmen are so Machiavellian; and, since the reports of the army debates at Putney were recovered at the end of the nineteenth century, we have been able to see that Oliver Cromwell, in spite of his changes of front in that year, consistently acted as a conciliator, attempting first to reconcile the army with parliament and then the King with the army; after that he tried hard to appreciate the point of view of the Levellers and to dovetail their constitutional proposals with those of Ireton, while upon his astute but tactless son-in-law he exercised a restraining influence. Since Fairfax never exerted the authority that was his, Oliver Cromwell assumed the political leadership of the army and desperately laboured to reconcile the Puritan factions with each other until, having failed, the new war came.

Chapter Seven

The Execution of Charles I

JOHN BUCHAN wrote that "what is called the Second
Civil War was, in England, strictly a royalist revolt".
It is perfectly true that what made the war so relentless
was that many Royalist officers, who had laid down their
arms on terms two years earlier, broke their oaths to fight
for their King again. But the broader historical significance of the second civil war was that—twelve full years
before the Restoration—this campaign foreshadowed that
alliance of Royalists and Presbyterians which was to put
an end to the Puritan Revolution. It also, as in 1660,
brought down an army from Scotland with the aim of
overawing London. Oliver Cromwell, always antagonistic
to Scottish interference with English affairs, said afterwards that the Royalists committed a "prodigious
treason" because the former quarrel on their part was that
Englishmen might rule over one another; this "to vassalize
us to a foreign nation".

The revolt, in fact, began in Wales, where a Presbyterian colonel, in command of the garrison of Pembroke, supported by other officers and soldiers who had fought for
the Parliamentarians in the first civil war, took up arms for
Charles I. Similarly in the navy, which had been Parliamentarian almost to a man, a Presbyterian vice-admiral
declared for the King and threatened the peace of London
by persuading about half the fleet to join the Royalist
revolt. In many other parts of the country the Cavaliers
received assistance or, at any rate, encouragement from
Presbyterians who had formerly been against them. All of
them hoped that an immediate invasion of the Scottish
Engagers would result in the restoration of the King, the

forcing of the Covenant on all and sundry, and the setting up of their religion exclusively.

In the spring of 1648 it looked, indeed, as if the cause of Cromwell and the New Model Army, and all the expectations of religious freedom and constitutional reform for which they had contended, were in deadly peril. Not only was South Wales aflame; the Royalists rose in Essex and Kent; to the north of England the towns that guarded the main roads from Scotland, Carlisle, and Berwick-on-Tweed were seized in the name of the King; two Yorkshire towns, Scarborough and Pontefract, also came under the control of the resurgent Cavaliers. Even London was menaced by the revolted warships. How far this was a genuine national reaction in favour of the King is not easy to gauge : one historian tells us that the rising was entirely popular in origin; another that "Englishmen in the mass remained neutral". It does seem probable that many ordinary people were disappointed because during the three years since the battle of Naseby no settlement had been attained between parliament and the King, while cracks had opened among the victorious Parliamentarians themselves, chiefly over questions of religion, but partly over political ideals. But, equally, divisions existed among the King's supporters in Scotland, and that was why the alliance with the Presbyterians failed to achieve its purpose now, as it finally did in 1660.

On the face of it, the position of the New Model Army was extremely precarious. For, while Fairfax had to turn to the south-east in order to suppress the Royalist risings there and Oliver Cromwell was ordered into South Wales where the war first began, only Major-General John Lambert, with a small cavalry force, was available in the north of England to protect the wide area where the Scottish assault was expected. Nevertheless, the English Puritan army had several advantages. The Royalist plans were ill-concerted and mistimed. In Scotland many of the Covenanters repudiated the engagements of their Commissioners; while the first Duke of Hamilton gathered an army together, the Marquis of Argyll, the most powerful single leader in Scotland, stood aside. Thus the experienced soldiers who had fought under the Earl of Leven at Marston Moor and elsewhere did not serve in the campaign, while the army which eventually invaded England consisted largely of raw recruits, inadequately armed. Secondly, the risings in England broke out before the Scots were ready, and as it happened, owing to the vigorous moves of Fairfax and Cromwell, the fires that burned in Wales and the south-east of England were largely quenched before the Scots even crossed the border. Finally, the New Model Army consisted of highly qualified and well-equipped men, who were smarting with a sense of grievance against both the Royalists, whom they regarded as having betrayed their word, and the Presbyterians, who had dubbed them "public enemies" for refusing to disband upon derisory terms. Cromwell himself was conscious of this depth of feeling, though he was chiefly incensed against the Scots, whom he had never trusted, and therefore accused the Royalists of a double crime in renewing the civil war as well as bringing in the Scots against the English Puritans.

It took Cromwell six weeks to obtain the surrender of Pembroke, partly because he had difficulty in collecting siege guns, some of them being wrecked at sea. As soon as the siege was over on 11 July, he led his men north to the assistance of General Lambert. This was one of the historic military marches : Cromwell and his men moved at the rate of ten miles a day in bad weather through partly hostile territory, and by the middle of August he was conferring with Lambert near Leeds.

Hamilton and the Scots had finally crossed the border on 8 July 1648, but, as he was awaiting reinforcements from Ireland and also lacked artillery and sufficient ammunition, his advance had been extremely leisurely. Lambert had originally taken up his position at Barnard Castle (where he had been joined by some of Cromwell's cavalry), on the borders of Durham and Yorkshire, as a precaution lest the Scots chose to switch east after moving through Cumberland in order to link up with their allies in Yorkshire. After some argument, however, the Scottish command had decided to come on through Lancashire, although it was not until after Cromwell and Lambert met that this important fact was understood. Both sides were enveloped in a fog of war and neither appreciated what the other was doing or how big their relative forces were. In reality, the Scots and Royalists together outnumbered Cromwell and Lambert by at least two to one.

But Cromwell was not much worried about numbers. He had a fine army which he could trust, and he knew that speed was the essence of victory. His forced march north gave him the initiative. Screened from the enemy by the Pennine chain, he decided to effect a surprise by leaving much of his artillery behind him and pressing through the Craven district of Yorkshire (where Lambert had been born), and along the valley of the Ribble towards Preston where the Scottish camp was thought to be. The Duke of Hamilton himself was at Preston, but though warned about Cromwell's approach—a report which he discounted—he sent his infantry on towards southern Lancashire, leaving only Sir Marmaduke Langdale with a small force of northern Royalists, supported by a few Scottish horse, to take the shock of Cromwell's assault upon a moor outside the town. Preston was a soldiers' battle, but weight of numbers and experience told.

After an heroic struggle the greater part of Langdale's infantry surrendered, while the bulk of the Scots and the contingent from Ireland stood almost within gunshot, doing nothing to help their afflicted comrades. The Scottish command, confused, surprised, and outmanoeuvred, then moved on through the night, first to Warrington and then to Wigan, where they intended to make a stand before joining their friends in Wales. Cromwell's army, though tired after its long marches and severe fighting, soon resumed the chase. At Winwick pass, near Warrington, a second battle was fought with the Scots, and thousands more prisoners were taken. The Duke of Hamilton himself, after vainly trying to reach Pontefract, laid down his sword on 25 August. The Scots from Ireland, a capable veteran force of some four or five thousand men under the command of Sir George Monro, having taken no part whatever in all these battles, eventually escaped over the border and on to Stirling.

Cromwell wasted no time in concluding what was perhaps the most striking of all his campaigns. He was at first concerned lest Monro should attempt to rescue the prisoners in Preston. But Monro had no such intention, and Cromwell marched unmolested to the Scottish frontier. His first task was to exact the surrender of Scottish garrisons left in Berwick and Carlisle. To enforce his demands he crossed the Tweed, and on 4 October entered Edinburgh. The Marquis of Argyll was only too pleased to come to terms with him in order to secure the support of the Ironside cavalry against his foes the Engagers, now concentrated in Stirling. So Argyll and his friends gladly promised Cromwell to ban the Engagers from all positions of trust, to disband Monro's army, and to surrender Berwick and Carlisle. Thus speedily were Charles I's hopes of rescue by his Scottish subjects dissipated. Cromwell left behind him three regiments to lend countenance to the new government of Scotland, and promptly returned to England. Sufficient problems awaited him there.

While the second civil war was being waged, the House of Commons, relieved of the presence of many Independent members like Cromwell, who were away fighting, still aspired, quite unprovoked by the Royalist revolt, to come to an agreement with the King. The day before the Duke of Hamilton surrendered, it repealed the "vote of no addresses" and a commission of fifteen members was sent to the Isle of Wight to reopen negotiations with Charles I. Included in this delegation was not only Denzil Holles, the principal Presbyterian leader in parliament, who had earlier fled from Westminster at the approach of the army, but also Cromwell's old friend and colleague, Sir Henry Vane. On his knees Holles begged the King to capitulate to the English Presbyterians' demands before the New Model Army should again bear down on London. Vane, on the other hand, pressed the King to concede the scheme for toleration envisaged in "The Heads of the Proposals". In these circumstances, the King, although he was already aware that the Engagers had been beaten by Cromwell, continued to hope that he could regain his throne by inciting his opponents to quarrel among themselves.

What the King failed to realize was that the parliamentary commissioners had little effective support behind them, apart from that of the Common Council of the City of London which was again clamouring for a Presbyterian settlement and the disbanding of the army. The Levellers, also influential in London, though not desiring power to fall into the hands of the "Grandees" of the army, stood for religious toleration and were antagonistic to the London Presbyterians, while John Lilburne had a scheme for balancing King and parliament against the army. Both the so-called Grandees and the Agitators in the army were growing increasingly restless. There is reason to suppose (though our knowledge about this is inadequate) that at this stage the influence of Cromwell's son-in-law, Henry Ireton, was decisive. Early in September, his regiment had protested against the repeal of "the vote of no addresses", and at the end of that month he himself sent a letter of resignation to General Fairfax. He offered to resign because he was strongly opposed to the reopening of negotiations with the King and had vainly urged upon the commander-in-chief the need again to purge the Commons of its Presbyterian leaders. Meanwhile the House of Commons had defiantly passed an ordinance imposing the Presbyterian system of Church government upon the whole of England, without any concessions whatsoever to toleration. Evidently, Fairfax soothed Ireton and promised that some action should be taken, for Ireton withdrew his resignation. Ireton's next move was to draw up a "remonstrance of the army" in which he demanded that no further negotiations should be conducted with the King but that he should be brought to public trial for renewing the civil war. Finally, Ireton entered into detailed discussions with the Levellers with a view to reaching a compromise between their schemes for constitutional reform and his own. Before Ireton determined to throw over the monarchy, however, he sent a message to Charles I giving him one last chance to make peace on the basis of the army's proposals. But the King still counted upon his enemies destroying each other, and plotted to escape from them.

Parliament, as well as the King, rejected the new scheme for a political settlement put forward by Ireton and fashioned by him out of the "Heads of the Proposals" and the Levellers' "Agreement of the People". This scheme for an extremely limited monarchy, one-chamber legislature, a more or less democratic electorate, and religious toleration represented the apogee of revolutionary political idealism.

As it was being evolved, Cromwell himself remained in the north of England, laying siege to Pontefract castle in Yorkshire, which was still in Royalist hands. It is by no means easy to guess from the evidence that survives exactly how his mind was working while his son-in-law was pickling his rod for the monarchy in London. What would the historian not give for a sight of the correspondence between him and Ireton that must surely have been carried on! Cromwell was clearly hesitating. "How easy", he wrote, "to find arguments for what we would have; how easy to take offence at things called Levellers, and run into an extremity on the other hand, meddling with an accursed thing" (i.e. further negotiations with an intractable King). Had they really to choose, he asked, between yielding to the King and accepting an all-embracing Presbyterianism? Was not the toleration of all godly people their proper aim? Thus he expressed himself early in November, showing that religious freedom was still his foremost concern. Gradually, however, he was converted to the view that the army itself was an instrument chosen by God to overcome the King and ensure that the fruits of war were not wasted. Yet, ever doubtful of the sanctification of force, he showed uncertainty. "Truly," he added as late as 25 November, even in putting forward this very suggestion, "these kind of reasonings may be but fleshly."

While Cromwell was searching his conscience in Yorkshire, Ireton was acting in the south. He, and not Cromwell, was then the resolute man, pressing forward Fairfax, rallying the New Model Army, trying to conciliate the Levellers, steeling his mind to desperate deeds. He had his way. The King was removed from the Isle of Wight; the army marched upon London; the Presbyterians were finally expelled from the Commons by the sword in what was known as "Pride's Purge"; and only a "rump" of some fifty members was allowed to remain. It was not until the night after "Pride's Purge" that Cromwell came back to London.

"Pride's Purge" had been carried out after the majority of the House of Commons had protested against the King's removal from the Isle of Wight, and had averred that it was still possible at this eleventh hour to negotiate with him as before. General Fairfax, we are told, regarded with disapproval and even horror the proposal that the House should be purged, yet allowed himself to be overruled in the Council of Officers by Henry Ireton supported by Colonel Thomas Harrison. Cromwell, for his part, was presumably consulted about the decision to march upon London, but not about the purge, which had to be rapidly determined. However, upon his arrival in the capital he said that he approved of it, and next day took his seat in the attenuated House.

During the next three weeks critical decisions about the future had to be taken by the small and resolute knot of men, of whom Cromwell and Ireton were the chief and who now had their hands upon the levers of power. They were under tremendous pressure, especially from the Levellers and from the rank-and-file of the army. Should the King be brought to trial and, if so, be sentenced to death? Or should other prisoners, who were also held responsible for bringing about the second civil war, such as the Duke of Hamilton, be tried first? We know that on 14 December Cromwell went to see Hamilton at Windsor, but, apart from that, the evidence upon those fateful days is sparse and contradictory. It is said, for example, that both on 21 and 25 December Cromwell appealed to his fellow officers for the King's life to be spared. But how could Cromwell foretell the verdict of a court? It has also been suggested that Cromwell imagined—being misled about the real character of Charles I—that the King would be willing to barter his life for the surrender of all but his formal powers as a monarch. Such chaffering with a man's life is hard to square with Cromwell's later defence of the King's execution as fundamentally an act of justice. It may be so, for the human mind is complex and in politics bargaining is the order of the day. Imaginative biographers seek, where the evidence tails away, to guess the answer, speculating on speculations. But only one thing is reasonably sure. Cromwell must have known that the trial and execution of the King would solve none of the immediate political difficulties. Its value was as an act of retribution and a terrible warning to the King's posterity. But it would not crush Royalism, for there was always another king.

The purged House of Commons passed an ordinance for bringing the King to trial on 1 January 1649. The ordinance in its final form provided for the appointment of 135 commissioners to act both as judges and jurors. When the court gathered in the Painted Chamber on 20 January, only sixty-eight of those nominated were present; John Bradshaw was the president. The King had been conducted from Windsor Castle to St. James's Palace on the previous day. Then he was taken by sedan-chair to Whitehall, moved by barge from Whitehall to the house of Sir Robert Cotton near the court, and afterwards escorted into Westminster Hall, whence the commissioners from the Painted Chamber assembled. These elaborate precautions were plainly designed to prevent a demonstration on the King's behalf. Bradshaw provided himself with a shotproof hat.

Bradshaw told the King that they were resolved to "make inquisition" for the innocent blood shed in the nation. When John Cook, as prosecuting counsel, stood up, the King raised his cane, telling him to "hold". The silver head of the cane fell off; after the King had vainly looked around for someone to pick it up, he did so himself and put it in his pocket. It was a sad and ominous beginning to the trial. The King asked by what power he was called upon to give answer to the charges of "high treason and other high crimes" preferred against him. "Remember," he said, "I am your lawful King." Bradshaw answered that they acted by the authority of the Commons of England, assembled in parliament, on behalf of the people of England who had elected him King. Charles I retorted that "England was never an elective kingdom" and that he himself was entrusted with the liberties of the people. Throughout the entire trial he refused to acknowledge the authority of the court or to plead to the charges.

On 23, 24 and 25 January, Cromwell and the other commissioners adjourned to the Painted Chamber and met in private session to examine witnesses. All that these could prove was that the King had led an army against parliament, which the commissioners knew already. By the third day the number of commissioners present had startlingly fallen to thirty-one. But the case against Charles Stuart having been proved to their satisfaction and the prisoner having been adjudged contumacious, since he refused to plead, a committee was appointed to draw up a sentence of death; next day this was accepted by the court; and on 27 January, sixty-eight commissioners went from the Painted Chamber to Westminster Hall where the King was brought to hear the sentence read. Fifty-nine commissioners—fewer than half those originally nominated—finally signed the death warrant. Cromwell, his mind made up, hesitated no more.

No delay was allowed in carrying out the verdict. On 29 January the King saw his thirteen-year-old daughter, Princess Elizabeth, and his ten-year-old son, Prince Henry, Duke of Gloucester, in St. James's Palace. His eldest son, Prince Charles, had sent a blank piece of paper to parliament offering to underwrite any terms that would save his father's life. The King asked for his dogs to be sent to the Queen, and refused all religious ministrations except that of a bishop, William Juxon of London. A scaffold was erected on the west side of the Banqueting House of Whitehall Palace. On 30 January, Charles I told one who attended him : "This is my second marriage day : I would be as trim today as may be; for before night I hope to be espoused to my blessed Jesus." The public executioner beheaded the King just before two o'clock. His body was buried a week later at Windsor in the falling snow.

In the end, King Charles I had, after all, been true to himself, obstinately defending the powers of the Stuart monarchy and the rights of the Church of England. He had been put to death by a ruthless oligarchy of some fifty or sixty men who honestly believed that they were performing an act of justice in the name of the English people. It is hard not to sympathize with this royal martyr, the central figure in that tragic scene. Three hundred years afterwards the German National Socialist leaders and generals were put on trial at Nuremberg for waging war, not, as King Charles had done, against their own people, but against other nations, and were condemned in the name of a newly fashioned international law. Those men were far greater villains than King Charles, though they, too, had struggled to uphold their own power in the name of the German people. King Charles I and Oliver Cromwell were, however, not modern demagogues but Christian gentlemen who both fought for what they conceived to be justice, liberty, and God's will. Plainly neither of them in any definable sense represented "the people of England". Yet other English kings, as John Bradshaw reminded Charles I—King John, King Henry III, King Edward II, King Richard II, and King Richard III—had been resisted, deposed, or killed because the great magnates of the realm had deemed them guilty of misgovernment. Now a wider class had used their swords and subjugated their King. That was the historic fact. The Puritan revolutionaries by their desperate act ultimately paved the way to constitutional government on a broader basis and, as will be argued, to wider religious liberties.

Oliver Cromwell had long hesitated about putting the King to death or even bringing him to trial. He was pushed on by Ireton, on the one hand, and by the Levellers on the other. But in Yorkshire he must have made up his own mind, after considering all the arguments and possibilities. What he learned on his return to London merely confirmed his decision. Testimony given after the Restoration, which must be suspect, nevertheless was unanimous in affirming that Cromwell was the man who in the end thrust through the execution of Charles I. But he did it in no spirit of anger or crude revenge. He saw himself as the instrument of justice, as did the judges at Nuremberg. Such terrible decisions are not often asked of men. To assess them in retrospect is easier than to make them at the time. Statesmen have to make them; historians to record them. Cromwell believed that only God could judge them.

93

Chapter Eight

The Birth of the Republic

AS we have seen, the men who brought the King to trial and execution had all of them been, until a year earlier, with one or two exceptions, monarchists. The rise of republicanism, as in the French Revolution, had come with a rush at the very last moment. But precedents and examples existed. Holland and Venice were already republics. To the educated country gentleman came the memory of what he had learned in the classics of Greek city-states and the early Roman republic. John Milton quoted with approval from Seneca :

> *"There can be slain*
> *No sacrifice more acceptable*
> *Than an unjust and wicked King."*

The Jesuits, preaching against Queen Elizabeth I in Cromwell's youth, had found historical instances in plenty to sustain the case for destroying an evil monarch; there is even a story of doubtful provenance that Cromwell himself now employed some of these jesuitical arguments in defending Charles I's execution to the Scottish Presbyterians. But the Independents, Fifth Monarchists, and other sectarians preferred to draw on examples from the Old Testament in justification of a republican government. Were the new rulers not the leaders of a Chosen People, who, like Moses and Aaron, had brought them towards the Promised Land?

But a flavour of democracy also attached to the settlement of the English Commonwealth. As early as 4 January 1649 the Commons had voted that "the people of England" were "the original of all just power, the Commons the supreme authority". This vote they ordered to be printed on the very day of the King's execution after the proclamation of his successor was forbidden. A great seal was inscribed with the words : "In the first year of freedom by God's blessing restored." In March, both the monarchy and the House of Lords were formally abolished; a High Court of Justice and a Council of State of forty-one members were set up, and finally, on 15 May, the establishment of a Free Commonwealth was approved by the House of Commons.

This democratic flavour owed much to the propaganda of the Levellers which had spread extremely swiftly since 1646, although among the Independents, too, demands for liberty and equality had been frequently heard. On 15 January, after long discussions between Lilburne and Wildman on one side, and Henry Ireton on the other, an amended "Agreement of the People" embodying a democratic constitution had been completed and was actually presented to parliament five days later. Cromwell himself had realized that nothing could be decided before the King's fate was settled, but the Levellers had insisted that a democratic system ought to have been perfected and set in motion before the King was deposed. This was never a practical possibility. However, the Levellers now expressed their disapproval of the King's execution (even though they had all wanted a republic and clamoured for his trial), and claimed that they had been "cheated and cozened." The oligarchic form of republican government that was constituted in the spring of 1649—although it was clearly only of a temporary character—met with virulent criticism from these eager idealists. They demanded forthwith a democratically elected single chamber to govern the country through executive committees, a written constitution, on the lines of their original, unamended "Agreement of the People", and guarantees for liberty in perpetuity.

No one happily reared in the comforts of liberal democracy can fail to be attracted by these advanced political conceptions of the Levellers. The difficulty then was that a democratically elected chamber would certainly have contained a substantial number of Royalists, and government by committee would not have worked. Thus the Commonwealth would have been split asunder before it had even come into being. The only way to prevent immediate anarchy was for a group of determined men to seize the reins of power, establish order, and ward off foreign foes. Indeed, such has been the pattern of all modern revolutions. That, more or less inevitably, was what happened then.

Cromwell was the first temporary chairman of the Council of State (later he was replaced by John Bradshaw), and Fairfax and others, who had not approved of the King's execution but promised to be loyal to the new Commonwealth, were allowed to become members. It was notable that Ireton, who more than any other man except Cromwell himself, was the engineer of revolution, and Thomas Harrison, the fanatical soldier who led the Fifth Monarchy men, though proposed, were both rejected for membership of the new Council. It was, paradoxically enough, a conservative body, still willing to persuade itself, in spite of the abolition of the Crown, the Church, and the House of Lords, that it was somehow governing according to the "fundamental laws" and restoring the ancient freedoms and liberties of the nation.

Naturally, the Levellers, headed by John Lilburne, were offended and attacked the new government, stirring up as much trouble as they could in the army. The Council of State, directed by Cromwell, would have none of that. Lilburne, who had uttered desperate threats, was put into prison, and one or two mutinies in the army were promptly suppressed by Fairfax and Cromwell. Indeed, this was one of the striking instances in history where the use of force overcame ideas. Within ten years of its foundation the Leveller movement, whose leaders were soon to stultify themselves by intriguing with the Royalist party abroad against the Commonwealth, was virtually dead, and the republicanism and democracy of the future were to draw their inspiration elsewhere.

The new republic was beset by many enemies. Abroad, general detestation was expressed at the beheading of an anointed King. So ambassadors were withdrawn from London, aid was provided for the Royalists in exile, though of a limited character, and English commerce was subjected to interruption by licensed pirates sailing not under the skull-and-crossbones but under the Royal Standard. The chief danger to the Commonwealth, however, came from Scotland and Ireland.

In Scotland the Covenanters took the view that whatever mistakes King Charles I might have made and however unwisely he had tried to undermine their religion, the English parliament and army had no right to put to death a Scottish king. They felt extremely uncomfortable about it, and had a guilty conscience, since it was they, after all, who in 1646 had handed over their monarch to the mercies of the rulers in London. But the Scots had not yet recovered from the beating that Hamilton's army had taken from Cromwell a year earlier; Argyll was still strengthening himself in power; and the danger from Scotland was not imminent.

In Ireland matters were different. Before the King's death the Lord Lieutenant Ormonde had concluded a treaty at Kilkenny with the Irish Catholic rebels. Members of the Irish Assembly in that town were invited to fight for the cause of justice, the Christian religion, and the sacred person of the King. When it heard this, the Assembly went wild with excitement and cheered "great Ormonde for ever". In the treaty, the Irish had been promised full security for their religion, but it was typical of the Royalist methods of negotiating about religion that Ormonde now proceeded to write to various English Protestant commanders in Ireland, secretly deprecating the supposed concessions to the Roman Catholic religion and inviting them to join his side. Ormonde had high hopes of driving the Puritan forces out of Ireland, and even of organizing an expeditionary force to invade England on the King's behalf. In May Ormonde, with a sizeable army, advanced upon Dublin, and another Royalist commander, Lord Inchiquin, captured Drogheda, north of Dublin. Meanwhile Owen Roe O'Neill, a handsome nationalist adventurer, nephew of the great Earl of Tyrone, threw in his lot with Ormonde and occupied Londonderry. The Puritan cause in Ireland seemed desperate.

To the new government in London, therefore, the re-conquest of Ireland appeared to be an urgent necessity. General Fairfax told the Council of State and parliament that the first need in organizing an expeditionary force was to appoint a suitable commander, and recommended Cromwell, who hesitated before he accepted the post. He demanded that adequate supplies and money should be allocated as a condition of his taking on the command. He was voted over 12,000 men and £100,000, and created Lord Lieutenant of Ireland with the fees attaching to that office. On 14 July he arrived in Bristol to prepare his base; while he was there he gave his secret blessing to a neutrality agreement which had been concluded between Owen O'Neill and a quiet ex-Royalist officer named George Monk. He also learned that Colonel Michael Jones, who had been in command at Dublin, had, with the aid of reinforcements sent from England, surprised and defeated Ormonde's army at the battle of Rathmines on 2 August. Thirteen days later Cromwell landed in Ireland, and promised to restore "that bleeding nation to its former happiness and tranquillity".

In spite of the victory at Rathmines, Cromwell had a large task before him. When O'Neill's agreement with Monk had expired he joined Ormonde's coalition, and the bulk of the country was under the control of the Royalists and native Irish. But Cromwell had many advantages. In the first place, the English navy commanded the sea, for Prince Rupert who, with a small fleet, had anchored at Kinsale in southern Ireland, was blockaded by Admiral Robert Blake and soon forced out; secondly, Cromwell's army was experienced and well led, and animated by a desire for revenge upon the native Irish, whom they re-garded as savage murderers of innocent Protestant people; lastly, the Royalists and Irish Catholics were not united. In fact, they distrusted and suspected one another, a state of feeling that was exacerbated by Cromwell's propa-ganda.

After securing Dublin, Cromwell at once marched north and laid siege to Drogheda. On 10 September he sum-moned the Royalist governor to surrender "to the end that effusion of blood may be prevented", and warned him that "if this be refused you will have no cause to blame me". But the governor decided to fight it out, defended the breaches blown in by Cromwell's artillery, and twice repulsed the assault columns with heavy losses. Cromwell himself led the third charge and carried the town. In fulfilment of his warning, he gave orders that all those found in arms in the town should be put to the sword. He himself estimated that about 2,000 men were killed, but it was probably fewer. It was an awful lesson to the other Irish garrisons, and though defensible in terms of war as it was waged on all sides in those times and long afterwards, it created a hateful memory in Ireland that never has been forgotten.

After the fall of Drogheda on 12 September, the Irish evacuated Dundalk, farther north, and Trim to the west, and Cromwell's main army turned south and besieged the port of Wexford that had long been a nest of pirates. When this town was summoned, the governor at first prepared to yield, but then, upon the receipt of reinforcements, changed his mind. Later the castle was betrayed, but the garrison resisted desperately in the streets of the town where there was much slaughter in which innocent citizens were killed. Cromwell was not himself directly responsible for the massacre there. From Wexford he moved on to New Ross and thence to Waterford. As winter drew on, the English soldiers were infected by dysentery and spotted fever. Cromwell himself was taken ill, and his health never really recovered from the campaign. His second-in-command who, as Colonel Jones, had won the battle of Rathmines, died of the plague and was replaced in effect by Cromwell's son-in-law, Ireton, who had accompanied him to Ireland. Meanwhile in Ulster O'Neill had died and much of the north had come over to the English Commonwealth. In the south Youghal, Kinsale, and Bandon also surrendered, so that most of the Irish coastline was in English hands. In the following year, Cromwell took Kilkenny and Clonmel with some difficulty, and in May handed over to Ireton before returning home under orders to England. Ireton soon occupied

Waterford, but afterwards the war degenerated into a series of raids and sieges.

Cromwell was essentially a humane man in his dealings with his fellow Christians, but the trouble was that from the beginning he treated the Irish as savages—much as the settlers in America regarded the Indians. He thought that first they must be subjugated by the sword and then given over to Protestant missionaries, English settlers, and a competent occupying garrison; and not until then did he believe that the country would settle down to a reign of equal laws, economic well-being, and sound religion. He was conscious of the cruelty of his action at Drogheda, for which he furnished apologies and explanations, and no doubt its calculated terror saved his soldiers' lives. But neither that, nor his wholesale condemnation of "popery" in a country which was essentially Roman Catholic, was likely to endear the Puritan Commonwealth to the Irish people. They suffered and remembered.

While Cromwell was away in Ireland, the Council of State and Rump Parliament which ruled England were not inactive. Their policy consisted of three parts. In the first place they aimed at introducing concessions to reformist ideals. John Milton, the poet who took office under the new government, had seen a vision of a "noble and puissant nation rousing herself like a strong man after sleep and shaking her invincible locks". Efforts were exerted to put the laws against poor debtors on a more merciful basis instead of allowing them to rot and starve; Fairfax's soldiers were ordered to clear the highways of robbers; attempts were made to ensure religious liberty, at least among the sects. Undoubtedly many people had been ruined by the long civil wars, unemployed ex-soldiers thronged the towns, trade suffered from interruptions, and commerce was damaged. Now the mass of the people acquiesced in the new government because they longed desperately for a period of peace, stability, and recovery. At the same time the government had to repress the lingering remnants of Royalism. A system of Press licensing was introduced, and gradually all news-sheets and pamphlets, except those favourable to the régime, were swept away.

Oaths of loyalty were required from officials, and the Presbyterian preachers were carefully watched. Lastly, certain specifically Puritan measures were enacted : adultery and fornication were subject to heavy penalties, and breaches in the observance of the Sabbath Day made punishable by fines.

But the new government was not particularly efficient. Since it was believed impossible to reconcile either the Royalists or the extreme Republicans, and since dangers from abroad still existed, security was the uppermost consideration in the minds of the new rulers. The practice whereby nearly every important question had to be tossed backwards and forwards between the Council of State and parliament did not make for smooth administration, and experience in the art of government was dearly bought.

The reason why Cromwell was recalled home from Ireland in May 1650 was because the danger from Scotland was acute and the loyalty of the commander-in-chief, General Fairfax, was suspect. King Charles II, who had assumed his title in exile in Holland, had at first pinned his hopes of restoration on the Irish, and later granted a commission to the Marquis of Montrose to raise forces on his behalf for use in Scotland, where he was named captain-general and later admiral. But Montrose, though a military genius, was a lone wolf with whom the dominant Covenanters under Argyll would have no dealings. The Covenanters were ready to accept Charles II as their king upon conditions, and when Cromwell was conquering the Irish, the King without a throne entered into negotiations with the Covenanters, reluctantly abandoning the loyal and heroic Montrose to his fate—he was hanged in Edinburgh as a traitor by his fellow Scots. In the blood of Montrose a treaty was signed, and in defiance of his father's memory, the young Stuart prince swore to uphold the Covenant and to impose Presbyterianism upon England. The Scottish Committee of Estates, the executive government, then began to organize an army to fight the English Puritans.

On Cromwell's return to London he was welcomed with enthusiasm. His victories in Ireland had raised the pres-

tige of the Commonwealth and disheartened the Cavaliers.
He was granted rewards of an income in confiscated lands,
and the use of a house which formed part of the palace of
Whitehall and known as the Cockpit. General Fairfax and
his other fellow Councillors of State greeted him in a
friendly way, and he himself was affable and modest. Immediately the question was debated what was to be done in
regard to Scotland. On 12 June 1650, parliament voted
that both Fairfax and Cromwell should go north. But
Fairfax was not keen; his support of the new government
had always been half-hearted. He was at best a conscientious policeman doing his duty. During Cromwell's
absence, he had strengthened the authority of the government by lengthy tours of the country. But he had refused
to take any oath of loyalty to the Republic and Charles I
had thought it worth his while to offer him the defunct
earldom of Essex (the same earldom had once been offered
by his father to Cromwell—earldoms were cheap gifts).
When parliament, confident that it was the intention of
the Scots to invade England, decided to give orders that
they should be forestalled, Fairfax declared that nothing
whatsoever would induce him to conduct an offensive war
upon a country with which a Solemn League and Covenant had been signed. Some consternation was displayed at
Fairfax's attitude, although it can hardly have been un-
expected : for Fairfax wielded real influence, especially in
the north of England; and he was trusted both by the
Independents and by the Presbyterians—indeed, no one
knew exactly where his own religious predilections lay. In
vain, Cromwell and others tried to persuade him to change
his mind. The dark and taciturn general laid down his
command on the nominal ground of ill-health, and at the
early age of thirty-eight retired to Yorkshire to grow roses.

Thus it was that Oliver Cromwell, who was now fifty-
one, was appointed captain-general and commander-in-
chief of the expedition to Scotland. He was already Lord
Lieutenant of Ireland, as well as being a member of parliament and of the Council of State. The Scottish campaign
was to be the final test of his military skill. The world was
still hostile to the Commonwealth. Prince Rupert was at sea

threatening the trade routes; Ireland was not yet completely subdued; the measures of the Rump Parliament had not satisfied many of the politically minded in the Puritan community; the Royalists, who had remained in England, being mulcted in their estates with heavy fines, had every urge to rise again should the Scots be victorious. Thus this was the crucial time for the Commonwealth, and all depended upon its new general.

Elaborate but hasty preparations were put in hand for the expedition. Troops were concentrated in the north of England; artillery was transported by sea; Thomas Harrison, now a major-general, was left in charge of the defence of England itself; and the shortest route, through Berwick-on-Tweed, was selected for the line of advance. Meanwhile, the Scots were also equipping themselves for the fray. The Covenanters' army was put under the command of David Leslie, an experienced professional soldier who had fought alongside Cromwell at the battle of Marston Moor. But since those Scots who had served with the "Engagers" in 1648 were banned from service, many of the soldiers raised by Leslie were relatively untrained, and whilst he had good hopes of exceeding the English army in numbers, he knew he could not equal them in quality, and relied upon defensive tactics, based on inner lines, to baffle his enemy. Leslie's strategy made nonsense of the claim of the English parliament that in the summer of 1650 the Scots were intending to invade England.

Cromwell crossed the border on 22 July, but was soon confronted by the difficulties of fighting against a capable general in command of a force imbued not only with some measure of national enthusiasm but also with that very Puritan spirit that had always animated his own army. He had a long supply line stretching back to Newcastle upon Tyne, and could not live on the country because it had been calculatedly laid waste. Leslie had fortified a line running west from Leith, and the Forth was another formidable obstacle. Although such clashes as took place between the English and the Scots demonstrated the superiority of the former, Cromwell found it impossible to thrust around the Scottish defences and menace Edinburgh or occupy Leith. Since the Commonwealth navy commanded the seas (Robert Blake was driving Prince Rupert from European waters), it was essential to hold a port where supplies could be landed. Thus eventually, at the end of August, Cromwell encamped his army at the port of Dunbar, some thirty miles from Edinburgh, embarked his sick and wounded, and defied his enemy to come at him. Leslie, after outmanœuvring Cromwell in the first weeks of the campaign, had followed him to Dunbar and deployed his army on Doon Hill, two miles south of Dunbar, thus threatening the road to England. It looked as if the Commonwealth army was cornered and would have to make its escape as best it could by sea; its numbers had been reduced to a mere 11,000 effectives, and the Scots had more than double that number. Well might Leslie have exclaimed, as Marshal Turenne is supposed to have done upon another occasion : "I have him now !" But it was not so.

The battle of Dunbar, which took place upon 3 September 1650, was in some ways a parallel to that very battle of Marston Moor in which Cromwell and Leslie had fought together. For just as at Marston Moor, Prince Rupert had occupied a defensive position and as evening came did not believe that his foes had any intention of attacking him, so, too, the Scots on the night of 2 September did not credit the idea that they would, in fact, be assaulted by Cromwell's inferior army. They actually came down off Doon Hill and extended their lines across the Dunbar–Berwick road towards the sea so as to be all the more certain of cutting off the English from their land route home. Cromwell and his generals decided upon a dawn offensive. The night was stormy and the moon obscured by squalls of rain. While the Scots crouched in discomfort amid the stooks of corn, the English, who had rested and been refitted in Dunbar, prepared for a surprise in the twilight. It was true that the original attack by six cavalry regiments on the Scottish right was hotly disputed, and when the infantry came in upon the centre, it too was thrust back by superior numbers; but Cromwell himself threw in his reserve of one cavalry regiment and three infantry regiments at the crucial moment and in the right place, and the confusion created by the original surprise was exploited and converted into overwhelming defeat. The Scottish left, cramped against the foot of Doon Hill, scarcely came into the battle at all, and, after an hour's struggle, was reduced to panic. Ten thousand prisoners were taken, and a few days afterwards the English occupied Edinburgh. The Scots withdrew to Stirling and the line of the Forth. As it was getting late in the campaigning season and Cromwell was still short of men and supplies, he contented himself with clearing his lines of communication and mopping up areas of resistance before winter closed in.

The defeat at Dunbar lowered the pride of the Scottish Covenanters. Hitherto, King Charles II, who had been graciously allowed to come to Scotland to watch the expected victory, had been kept in humiliating tutelage. Now, on 1 January, 1651, he was crowned King at Scone, put in nominal command of the Scottish army while the help of out-and-out Royalists was welcomed. On the other hand, this had the effect of dividing the Covenanters. Some of the more rigid Scottish Presbyterians attributed their defeat at Dunbar to the fact that they had fought for a "malignant" King, tainted by all sorts of doubtful religious affiliations. Cromwell's experts in political warfare (at which he was no mean hand himself) put out proclamations aimed at alienating the Covenanters, their fellow Puritans, from the Royalists or "men of blood". It is said that this propaganda played its part in bringing about the surrender of the virtually impregnable Edinburgh castle and gaining an English victory in the Glasgow area. Yet the winter was severe, Cromwell himself was taken ill, and Leslie, counting upon Scottish patriotism rather than religious excitement, was a resourceful enemy. During the summer a series of probing attacks and attempts to outflank Leslie's lines and compel him to fight again all proved abortive. Moreover, the danger existed that if Cromwell threw the bulk of his army across the Forth, the road to England would be exposed, and that King Charles II, relying upon his supporters

there to revolt in large numbers, would gladly march along
it.

The significance of the Worcester campaign, which
was in fact the concluding phase of Cromwell's war in
Scotland, was that Cromwell deliberately chose to face this
last danger. No one can doubt that he was fully aware of
the strategic possibilities. Cromwell had allowed his lieutenant-general, Charles Fleetwood, to return to London
precisely in order to marshal a new militia which would be
at hand to reinforce him if the Scots broke through. He
also knew that his own highly trained cavalry was capable
of overtaking the Scots once they left their bases and ad-
ventured across the border. His only problem was how to
make the Scots budge from their entrenched positions.

On 17 July 1651, Colonel Robert Overton managed to
slip a brigade across the Forth at Queensferry and obtain
a lodgement on the northern bank. Once that success was
achieved, Cromwell sent his best general, John Lambert,
with a large force in Overton's wake. On 20 July Lambert
fought the battle of Inverkeithing, routing the troops that
Leslie detached to meet him. Cromwell at once determined to push the bulk of his army over the Forth and to
seize Perth, thereby cutting off Leslie from his supplies.
Directly the English move on Perth was known in the
Scottish camp, King Charles II ordered an advance into
England. It is doubtful if Leslie approved of this, for his
heart was never in the Worcester campaign. The real
commander of the invasion of England was the second
Duke of Hamilton, who thus followed in the doomed footsteps of his executed brother, like him marching down
through Lancashire to die for a Stuart king.

The campaign went entirely according to Cromwell's
expectations. Within a month of King Charles II's crossing
the border on 6 August, all was over. Major-General
Thomas Harrison, who had earlier been summoned by
Cromwell into Scotland for consultation, was waiting at
Newcastle in case the invaders should take the eastern
road; Lambert, with four or five thousand picked cavalry,
went in swift pursuit of the Scots; and Harrison soon joined
him in Lancashire. There they might have defeated the

King, but Cromwell wanted to crush him completely and so bring the civil wars to their conclusion. Once the Scots tired, they were bound to be caught. They were surrounded in Worcester at the beginning of September. The young King put up a splendid fight against odds, and succeeded in making his own escape after many adventures, sailing in mid-October from Brighton to join his mother in France. But his followers and the Scots paid the full penalty of defeat. James Stanley, seventh Earl of Derby, of a family ever loyal to the throne, who had rallied to King Charles II in Lancashire, was executed, leaving his wife in command of the garrison of the Isle of Man. The second Duke of Hamilton died of his wounds at Worcester. Four thousand Scottish prisoners were sent to London to subsist on biscuits and cheese in captivity, and Scotland itself became an occupied country. Cromwell, having written his dispatches, rode south in a leisurely manner, was greeted enthusiastically by a parliamentary delegation at Aylesbury, and then "went a little out of the way a-hawking".

Within three years of King Charles I's death, the Commonwealth of England, Scotland, and Ireland had been firmly established.

Chapter Nine

Cromwell and the Dissolution of the "Rump" Parliament

OLIVER CROMWELL was in his fifty-third year when he returned to London after the battle of Worcester. There is a story that he said at this time that if he had been ten years younger he would have made the world tremble. It does not sound in the least like Cromwell, and in fact we have a letter of his written one month after Worcester in which he asked in some perplexity : "How shall we behave ourselves after such mercies?" and stressed his own "weakness" and "inordinate passions". It is true that in his disposition was the strain of a Protestant crusader. He had been an admirer of Gustavus Adolphus, the Swedish hero of the Thirty Years War, and he might later, had other things been equal, have fought alongside a successor of Gustavus Adolphus, the brilliant young Charles X, if the Swedish king had been willing to turn his arms against the Catholic Habsburgs. But in the years that remained to him, Cromwell's health was never good; he had been seriously ill both during the Irish and Scottish campaigns. Living in Whitehall Palace close to the poisonous stench of town and Thames, he missed the country air that he had breathed in his young days in the fenlands; he took regular exercise by the river at Hampton Court, but too soon the prison-house of duty in London closed upon him.

After Worcester he became a wealthy man. Hampton Court Palace, as well as the Cockpit, was assigned to him as a residence, where he lived with his family and friends. Besides his pay as commander-in-chief (amounting to £10 a day), he was voted £4,000 a year out of confiscated

Royalist estates, and acquired, among other properties, nineteen houses in the Strand. Not only did he give a substantial part of his income to charity, but on more than one occasion he waived a portion of his salary in the public interest. For example, once he left Ireland he never took any of his pay as lord lieutenant. Still, he had to adapt himself to a new scale of values, and his two younger daughters married better than their sisters, into the aristocracy, and received large dowries.

Three women mattered to Oliver Cromwell, his mother, his wife, and his second daughter, and they were all named Elizabeth. (The example of the great Queen Elizabeth influenced him, too, so far as public policy went.) His mother he visited every night when he was at home. When she was ill he did not care to leave her. Her death, though she lived to the ripe age of eighty-nine, was a grave blow to him. One may hazard the guess that he owed much of his religious faith and also of his liberal attitude of mind to her (for women are, as a rule, more tolerant than men; at any rate, they do not need books of political theory to convince them of the virtues of being charitable). The doctrine that the English were God's people seems to have been ingrained in her. Cromwell's wife is a somewhat less distinct figure, and she was not a little abashed by her husband's greatness. She accompanied him to Dublin during his campaign in Ireland, which, in view of the English belief in the savagery of the Irish, showed courage : when he was away from her they corresponded frequently, though few of their letters have survived; in one of them he said : "Indeed, I love to write to my dear, who is very much in my heart."

His children were treated, as successful men are liable to treat their children, with a mixture of strictness and spoiling. Owing to the wars he did not often see his sons as they grew to manhood. Two of them died young; the other two, Richard and Henry, had sharply contrasting characters. Richard was gentle and idle, with little ambition other than to live the life of a country gentleman, to go hunting, and to marry the girl he loved. Henry had the makings of a soldier and a statesman; the report he brought home when he first visited Ireland in his twenties had all the stamp of mature judgment. But he was never a popular figure; because of his very astuteness men were jealous of him, and he was always at loggerheads with his brother-in-law, Lieutenant-General Charles Fleetwood. Neither of Oliver's sons inherited the religious enthusiasm of their father, who once observed that "often the children of great men have not the fear of God before their eyes". His letters to them, usually expressing anxiety over their spiritual welfare, were a little schoolmasterish in tone. Like other fathers, he forgot they had grown up.

To his four daughters he was tender and considerate. His eldest, Bridget or Biddy, was like her father in looks and in faith. She was married first to Ireton, who died fifteen months after Cromwell had left him in Ireland, and then to Fleetwood, who had been lieutenant-general in Cromwell's expeditionary army in Scotland. Both of them were keen Puritans, but Fleetwood had neither Ireton's brains nor character. It was a loss to Oliver when the weaker Fleetwood replaced Ireton as his eldest son-in-law. Elizabeth was her father's pride and joy. Even in the indifferent portraiture of that time, she comes down to us as a beautiful and attractive woman. She does not seem to have been lucky in her husband, whom the censorious Lucy Hutchinson called "a debauched, ungodly Cavalier"; but she was fortunate both in her children and her friends, and when her father became Lord Protector she was said to have "acted the part of a princess very naturally". She had a wit and a gaiety that lightened the Puritan Court, but one may take a pinch of salt with popular stories of her Royalist sympathies. Outside his family, there were no other women in Cromwell's life; Royalist anecdotes about this, as about his youthful wickednesses, do not bear impartial investigation.

Although only three or four genuinely independent portraits of him exist, Cromwell's face is familiar to all who have an interest in British history. His long hair, his piercing eyes, his big nose ("Coppernose", the Royalists nicknamed him), his strong chin, go to make up what has recently been called a typical English face. He was just under six feet tall, had an eloquent voice and, in his younger days, a reddish complexion. He bore himself with a natural dignity, but was easily accessible. He never talked to his intimates or even his petitioners, as public men are so often accustomed to do, as if he were addressing a public meeting, and though he always struggled to interpret the will of God to himself, he never spoke to others with the voice of God. His worst fault—he admitted it to himself— was his temper, which he lost rather easily when he was young, though later he had it under better control. His finest virtues were his humaneness and his tolerance. The man who ordered the slaughter of the garrison at Drogheda, or the dismissal of two parliaments by the sword, was infinitely tender towards those who suffered. Many of his letters that have come down to us are concerned with helping his old soldiers and assisting their widows. Again, the same man who was brutal in condemning the public celebration of the Mass in Ireland, loathed any kind of religious intolerance in England, and in the end, at the height of his supremacy as Protector, permitted the holding of Communion according to the rites of the Church of England, or even of the Mass in many private houses in London.

Like his sons, Oliver, if he could have had his private wishes, would have preferred the life of a country gentleman to ruling in state from Whitehall. But his deep sense of duty, both to his God and to the community, never left him in any doubt that his retirement was impossible. So he had to make do with a second-best. He hunted and hawked but, unlike King James I and King Charles I, he never allowed his devotion to sport to keep him long from the affairs of State. At Hampton Court he had fish ponds built, and he welcomed gifts of horses from foreign rulers, though he also purchased many himself. Horses were his abiding passion, and it is said that he possessed the finest stud in the land. But he would not tolerate bear-baiting or cock-fighting, or cruelty to animals in any form. "He was naturally compassionate to objects in distress," wrote his steward, "even to an effeminate measure."

In most of his personal tastes Cromwell was essentially

English. What he liked best for a meal, it is said, was roast beef and ale; he did not care for foreign kickshaws upon the table. But he was not averse to a glass of wine. Shakespearian "sack" was on tap when he entertained guests, and when he gave a large party he would provide music and French wine. He appreciated both instrumental and vocal music, particularly the organ and motets. And he enjoyed smoking his pipe and an occasional game of bowls.

Nothing is more misleading than to think of Oliver Cromwell as a stern unbending Puritan. Historians sometimes insist that he was less popular with his soldiers than Fairfax and Lambert, but there is little basis for this; on the contrary, many pieces of evidence suggest that Cromwell's humanity and accessibility were widely recognized, and that he was no stricter disciplinarian than any other officers of his day. It is true that a sentence has often been quoted from a pamphlet written in 1649 in defence of an incipient army mutiny entitled, *The Hunting of the Foxes from Newmarket and Triploe Heaths to Whitehall by Five Small Beagles late of the Army*; these were five rebellious troopers whom Cromwell had cashiered. The sentence claimed that Cromwell was an arrant hypocrite who would "weep, howl and repent, even while he doth smite you under the first rib". Why such interested testimony to his hypocrisy should be quoted as conclusive evidence by responsible authors is hard to fathom. He was also freely accused by the Levellers of aspiring to kingship. But in Cromwell's letters and speeches it is possible to follow the actual working of his mind, the doubts, the hesitations, the weighing of arguments, the final and often reluctant decisions. He may sometimes have been deluded as to what was right and wrong—which human being is not?—but that was not hypocrisy. Cromwell had never promised the Levellers that after the death of the King they should enjoy full-scale democracy; he never pretended that the wishes of the rank-and-file of the army should determine the future shape of government. If they thought he had done so, it was they who deceived themselves. If they imagined that his highly individual and emotional religion was a cover for purely personal ambition, their disappointment over their failure to realize their radical aims blinded them, for even their leader, John Lilburne, had recognized Cromwell's integrity.

Cromwell's chief faults were his quick temper, his slowness in making up his mind, and his habit, in later years, of giving way too easily to others. Though he was no doctrinaire, his mind worked with little formal reasoning in the service of God's people, "the apple of His eye". His political genius was intuitive : he mulled over the facts, digested the lessons of experience, waited to see if there were any change in circumstances, and then came to his ultimate resolve. He did not afterwards ask his advisers to explain to him why he had done so, for, being a devout Christian, he believed his guidance was providential. He was sure that life had a purpose and that it could be seen working in history. He thought that each individual must find out the Truth for himself. But once he was converted he never doubted—such was the prevalent Calvinist climate of his lifetime—that he was indeed one of God's elect, destined to serve Him to the end.

The position of the English Commonwealth had immensely brightened by the close of the year 1651. Before he died, Henry Ireton had secured the surrender of Limerick, and only mopping-up operations were needed in Ireland. In Scotland her leaders were shattered and divided; her best soldiers were prisoners. Major-General Monk, whom Cromwell left behind, set about ruthlessly completing the military victory. The Isle of Man, the Channel Islands, and the Scillies, the last outposts of Royalism, had been reduced to obedience. The Spanish government, which had been one of the first to recognize the new republic, sought an English alliance in its war against France; while France, though it delayed recognition, began putting out feelers for a *détente* and contemplated hiring Cromwell's Ironsides to fight the Spaniards in the Netherlands. Prince Rupert who, after being driven from Southern Ireland had found a base in Portugal, was driven out and chased away from the Mediterranean by Robert Blake. The Dutch, who had benefited by the civil wars and the general confusion to extend their commerce and shipping business throughout the world, were brought to an abrupt halt by Acts passed by the English parliament restricting their right to trade with the British colonies or to bring foreign imports to British ports in their ships.

Cromwell now believed that the time had come to establish the Commonwealth on a firm footing and to restore domestic peace. He pressed hard for an Act of Amnesty for the Royalists, later resenting the many exceptions with which the Act was clogged; he voted for mercy to be shown both to the Earl of Derby and to Sir Charles Cavendish, taken in arms, but he was overruled. But he wanted more than amnesty : he advocated the calling of a new parliament to replace the Rump, he sought a final ecclesiastical settlement, and he urged domestic reforms. In his dispatch after the battle of Dunbar, he had written to the Speaker : "Relieve the oppressed, hear the groans of poor prisoners in England; be pleased to reform the abuses of all professions; and if there be anyone that makes many poor to make a few rich, that suits not a Commonwealth." After Worcester, he begged that "justice and righteousness, mercy and truth, may flow from you, as a thankful return to our gracious God".

Parliament began at once to reduce the size of the army, including the garrisons in Scotland and Ireland, and to dispose of the prisoners that had been taken. Many of these prisoners were shipped overseas, either to the West Indies or to New England as indentured servants. It must not be supposed that they were sold into slavery or ill-treated. Indeed, Cromwell's friend, the Reverend John Cotton of Boston, wrote to him that the prisoners in Massachusetts worked three days a week for their masters and had the other four days to themselves; they had been promised their freedom as soon as the masters had been paid for their investment. But parliament made very little progress in promoting these social reforms that had been adumbrated in Cromwell's dispatches. Cromwell was slowly reaching the conviction that as long as the present form of government continued in which some fifty over-worked politicians virtually staffed both the national legislature and the national executive, no real advances were to be expected.

Cromwell himself had pressed from his place in the House of Commons in the autumn after Worcester that the existing House of Commons should forthwith be dissolved and another elected in its stead. A number of the members were ready to enlarge the House, but were quite unwilling to give up their own seats, while they demanded the right to approve any new members who might join them. Eventually, on 18 November 1651, a compromise was reached in the House. A date for a dissolution was fixed three years later (in November 1654), but the existing members gave up their claim automatically to retain their seats in the next House. Cromwell accepted this compromise reluctantly : "He had been talking loudly not only of popular reforms but also of executing justice without respect of persons"—that is to say, of uncovering corruption—and in December he summoned a meeting of lawyers and army officers at the house of the Speaker to examine the possibility of strengthening the executive. But nothing came of this, and during 1652 the country was absorbed in the Dutch war.

This war arose more or less accidentally, but it was brought about by a variety of causes. There were a number of political grievances, some of them long-standing, such as the massacre of English traders at Amboyna in 1624, and the support the Dutch Republic had lent to the Royalists in 1649, when Prince Rupert had been afforded shelter for his ships and King Charles II had been given a refuge from which to negotiate with the Scots. Above all stood a business rivalry which waxed throughout the century : squabbles over the herring fisheries, rivalries over the carrying trade, disputes over colonies; most important, arguments about international law, the Dutch claiming that English warships had no right to seize enemy goods carried in neutral ships, unless they were specifically contraband. The Dutch disliked the English Navigation Act of 1651, which forbade foreign ships to carry goods to England unless they came from the country where the goods originated; but even more they objected to the judg-

ments of the English Admiralty Courts, which freely confiscated cargoes carried in Dutch ships, allegedly belonging to hostile nations, seized by privateers under letters of
reprisal issued to them. So the war broke out, and in its
early months the Dutch fully held their own. The English
fleet was bigger and its sailors more experienced, but
though both sides had excellent admirals, the Dutch were
throughout at a disadvantage. The English, it was said,
could attack a mountain of gold, the Dutch a mountain of
iron. The war was not specially popular in Puritan England—the Dutch, after all, were fellow Protestants—and
the opposition to it was strongly expressed in the army.
Cromwell, as commander-in-chief and as a member of the
Council of State, played a leading part in the war, but in
private he made no secret of his dislike for it. It was another factor that turned him against the ruling parliamentary oligarchy, though its leaders included such old friends
of his as Henry Vane and Oliver St. John.

Another question over which Cromwell showed some
dissatisfaction in 1652 was that of reforming the Church.
Although the bishops had been abolished and in 1648 an
ordinance for establishing Presbyterianism had been
passed, the power of the Independents and Sectarians was
such that the matter had been set on one side until the final
end of the civil wars. In February 1652, Cromwell was
appointed by parliament a member of a committee for the
propagation of the Gospel. To this committee, Dr. John
Owen, an Independent minister who was Cromwell's
chaplain in Ireland, submitted proposals for the re-establishment of the Church. This Church was to be controlled,
instead of by the bishops, by two bodies known as Triers
and Ejectors. The Triers were to approve the admission of
preachers, the Ejectors to remove unfit ministers and
schoolmasters. Outside this Church, other Christian sects
were to be permitted to hold services, provided that they
gave notice of their meeting places to the local magistrates.
Owen and his supporters added a list of fifteen Christian
fundamentals which they insisted must be accepted by all
inside and outside the endowed Church or be excluded
from toleration. In Cromwell's view these restrictions went

too far : "I shall need no revelation", he said, "to discover unto me the man who endeavours to impose upon his brethren"; and again : "I had rather that Mahometanism were permitted amongst us than that one of God's children should be persecuted." Other members of the committee thought, on the contrary, that Owen's plan was too liberal; again a settlement was shelved.

Not only did the committee on religion make no progress, but later an Act for propagating the Gospel in Wales was not renewed, much to the indignation of Cromwell (himself of Welsh descent) and of Thomas Harrison, who was a leading figure in the administration of the Act. Another committee, which was set up to reform the law, achieved little progress and was bogged down, as Cromwell related afterwards, with defining the word "encumbrances". In August 1652 the army leaders began to express their impatience with the dilatoriness of parliament's proceedings. Not only was the need for reforms in the government, the law, and the Church pressed, but demands for granting arrears in pay to the soldiers were reiterated and the election of a fresh House demanded. Cromwell persuaded the Army Committee to omit the last demand from its petition as presented, and the House of Commons responded by appointing a fresh committee to draw up a Bill for new elections at some unspecified future date (thus abandoning the previous decision to dissolve in November 1654).

Why did the compromise of August 1652 fail to work? How did it come about that within eight months the army forcibly dissolved parliament? Unquestionably a deep distrust prevailed between army and parliament, which became accentuated as the months rolled on. During this crucial period Cromwell himself acted as a conciliator; he arranged and attended meetings representative of both sides in the search for an agreed political solution. But he felt that the discontent with the government of the country was not merely confined to the army. "We found," he said later, "the people dissatisfied in every corner of the nation." Moreover, he admitted in private that he shared his fellow-officers' suspicion of the civilian members of the

House : "As for the Members of Parliament [he told the lawyer Bulstrode Whitelocke in November 1652], the army begins to have a strange distaste for them, and I wish there were not too much cause for it; and really their pride and ambition and self-seeking, ingrossing all places of honour and profit to themselves and their friends, and their daily breaking forth into new and violent parties and factions; their delay of business and design to perpetuate themselves, and to continue power in their own hands; their meddling in private matters between party and party, contrary to the institution of Parliament, and their injustice and partiality in those matters, and the scandalous lives of some of the chief of them; these things do give much ground for people to open their mouths against them and to dislike them. . . ."

In addition to all that, the Dutch war, in which the army played little part, was not going too well, and Tromp, the great Dutch admiral, was still at liberty to range the English Channel.

Cromwell himself was under enormous pressure. On the one hand, the extremists in the army, led by Thomas Harrison, were pushing him on to dissolve the Rump Parliament; on the other, the proposal was mooted to replace him as commander-in-chief either by Lambert or by Fairfax. Yet in the spring of 1653 Cromwell still ardently hoped for another compromise : that the Rump would voluntarily dissolve itself so as to allow a more energetic government and legislature to be chosen. Evidently he had expectations of support from his old friend, Sir Henry Vane, who, like him, was tolerant in his religious opinions, had been opposed to Scottish intervention in English affairs, and disliked the Dutch war. Vane was not in favour of dissolving parliament but of transfusing it with fresh blood. Harrison and Lambert in the army, however, wanted government by a temporary committee or commission while a new constitution was drawn up. On 19 April a conference met at Cromwell's lodgings in Whitehall at which Vane was present, and both sides put their points of view. Hard things were said, but when the meeting was wearily adjourned, it was understood that no final decision was to be reached in the House without the approval of the army.

Nevertheless, the very next day Vane and his friends at once started pushing through a Bill which was believed to aim at the perpetuation of their own power. The guiding light was Sir Arthur Haselrigg, a proud and wealthy northern magnate, of republican opinions and limitless ambitions. It was he who must have persuaded Vane to go back on his undertaking of the night before, whatever it was—and that may, in any case, have been misunderstood by Cromwell. When Cromwell heard the news, he was furious : "He flamed up in wrath against the promise-breakers", and went down to the House, dressed as he was, accompanied by a guard of soldiers, to see what was happening. He charged the House, as soon as he had an opportunity to speak, with all the faults that he had earlier described in his conversation with Whitelocke, its injustices and delays, the corruption or self-interest or sinister interests bearing upon it. "Perhaps you think this is not parliamentary language?" he exclaimed. "I confess it is not. . . ." Then he accused individual members by name of scandalous conduct, and finally he called in the guard to dissolve the House. Vane protested and Cromwell turned on him, his old friend and colleague, in sorrow and anger : "O Sir Henry Vane !" The mace, symbol of the Speaker's authority, was taken away at Cromwell's orders ; the Bill on elections was snatched from the clerk ; the members were thrust out, and the doors were locked.

That same afternoon Cromwell attended the Council of State which he himself, in terms of votes, was the principal member : John Bradshaw, who had presided at the trial of King Charles I, was in the chair. Cromwell informed those present that parliament had been dissolved and that the existing Council of State had come to an end with it. Bradshaw replied to him in famous words : "Sir, we have heard what you did in the House the morning, but before many hours all England will hear it. But, sir, you are mistaken to think that parliament is dissolved, for no power under heaven can dissolve them but themselves. Therefore take notice of that."

John Buchan wrote that "by the impulsive act of that April morning, Oliver made the second great blunder of his career", the first being the execution of King Charles I. Sir Charles Firth noted that "with its expulsion [of the Commons] the army flung away the one shred of legality with which it had hitherto covered its actions. . . . Henceforward Cromwell's life was a vain attempt to clothe that force in constitutional forms. . . ."

To destroy is easy; to rebuild much harder. Cromwell had indeed convinced himself that the Rump was being unfaithful to the real purposes of the Puritan Revolution and that some other kind of government was necessary to promote reforms in Church and State. But he himself was an old parliamentarian—he had fought for parliament against the King—and it was never his intention permanently to replace the House of Commons by either a military dictatorship or a Puritan oligarchy. The trouble was that, once parliament had thus been forcibly dissolved by the army, harmony among the victors in the civil war was irreparably damaged. No doubt it had been injured much earlier, perhaps at the time of Pride's Purge or when the New Model Army first marched upon London. It was not Cromwell who set the example of intimidating parliament. But from now on, in spite of all Cromwell's own well-intended efforts to mend matters, the breach between the parliamentary lawyers and the country gentlemen, on the one side, and the republican Puritan soldiers, on the other, was never healed. Because of that, many blossoms of the revolution were doomed to bear no fruit.

Chapter Ten

Cromwell and the Shape of Government

WHILE at the beginning of the seventeenth century constitutional lawyers insisted that the King in parliament was more powerful than the King out of parliament, the House of Commons by itself still occupied a relatively modest place in the scheme of national government. Its chief strength was that it was required to vote taxes when asked by the Crown, and if it was so asked, its petitions and grievances were naturally heard with greater respect. But because, except in times of war, Queen Elizabeth I had been able to live upon her own hereditary revenues, she had not often needed to call upon the House to grant her subsidies. Early in his reign, King James I had warned the House that as it derived its privileges from him it must not use them against him; he instructed a later House that it must not meddle with his government or plumb the deep mysteries of State. King Charles I affirmed, as late as 1626, the "Parliaments are altogether in my power for their calling, sitting and dissolution; therefore, as I find the fruits of them good or evil, they are to continue or not to be".

Yet the constitutional history of the last sixty years of the century consisted largely of the rise of the House of Commons to a dominant position in the government of the kingdom. This had never before been its accepted role. In the past, parliaments had been called at irregular intervals and only sat for a few weeks at a time. In looking at the history of the mid-century, then, we must not think in terms of our own lifetime when the House of Commons is fully representative of the nation, is in session for the larger part of the year; when its members are paid, and when it furnishes the bulk of the Cabinet that rules the country. Even when King Charles I was compelled to assent to a Triennial Act in 1641, he committed himself only to calling a parliament once every three years : the responsibility for the actual government was still entirely his and his ministers. The victory of parliament over the King in the civil wars, which lasted intermittently from 1642 to 1651, had thus produced a totally new state of affairs.

Though the Commons then temporarily became the focus of government, ever since "Pride's Purge" in 1648, the House had been in no sense a representative body, and as the executive Council of State had been completely subject to it, in fact an oligarchy of a somewhat fortuitous character had come to rule the country according to no known or even clearly prescribed constitutional procedure. And so, when Cromwell and the army overthrew the Rump in 1653, they reckoned that they were now in possession of a clean slate on which to rewrite the English constitution.

The question was : What should that new constitution be? One more realist set of Cromwell's advisers simply wanted to set up a small *ad hoc* body to rule the country for the time being and meanwhile to frame a new written scheme of government; another, more idealist, thought that they must accept the logic of the Puritan revolution and envisaged a theocratic assembly to govern, representative solely of the chosen godly people or the "honest party" which had won the war. But in 1653, as in 1649, no carefully thought-out scheme of government was in existence, or at any rate generally accepted in the army, ready to replace the incomplete parliamentary system that had been destroyed. "It was necessary to pull down this government," it was said, "and it would be time enough then to consider what should be placed in the room of it." Cromwell later observed that since his own authority as commander-in-chief was the sole "constituted authority" now left in the nation, he could if he wished have proceeded to rule as a "single person". But he deliberately did not choose to do so : he was never an autocrat by temperament. Instead, the Council of the Army selected 140 persons (including eleven representing Scotland and Ireland) out of a list nominated by the congregational churches both to legislate and to direct the government. When this assembly met, Cromwell told the members that it had been decided "not to grasp the power ourselves, to keep it in military hands . . . but to divest the sword of the power and authority in the civil administration", and put the government in their hands. Cromwell was persuaded that these excellent religious enthusiasts—"Saints" as they were nicknamed—who were in fact for the most part lesser gentry, tradesmen, and schoolmasters, would form the basis of an ideal Puritan administration. But afterwards he came to regard this "Little Parliament" as a tale of his own "weakness and folly".

The trouble was that most of these worthy men, who were different in character, background, and experience from the Rumpers, though inflamed and inspired by daring radical notions, were totally inexperienced in the art of government. It was as if a group of Congregational ministers or a chamber of commerce was suddenly invited to clear all the in-trays of Whitehall. They were also inflated with a sense of their own new importance. They improperly took the name of parliament; they refused to bring the Dutch war to an end, except upon humiliating terms for their enemies; they thrust the Leveller leader back into prison; they rejected Dr. Owen's carefully thought-out scheme for ecclesiastical reform, while at the same time they offended the once predominant Presbyterians; extreme Fifth Monarchy men ruled the committees of the Assembly; and the general who had called them to office was studiously ignored. In a word, the Saints, like most *parvenus*, made themselves unpopular all round, and Cromwell and Lambert were eventually driven to the conclusion that they must break with their former colleague, Major-General Thomas Harrison, who was the chief architect of this "Assembly of Saints", and think again.

The third scheme of government tried during the Interregnum was more elaborately planned. John Lambert, who was not merely a very good general but an educated political thinker, had during 1653 drawn up a constitution, known as "The Instrument of Government", which embodied the political ideals of the higher ranks of the army. Under this constitution the electoral constituencies were made more equal, but the franchise was so restricted that parliamentary representatives were bound to be drawn from the wealthier middle classes. Parliament was to meet only once every three years for a minimum period of five months, and then, as of old, chiefly for legislative purposes. The executive power was placed in the hands of a Lord Protector, assisted and guided by a Council of State. The aim of this constitution was to provide stable government, to impose a system of checks and balances within it, and to guarantee the inviolability of both religious liberty and private property. The functions of parliament were thus greatly reduced compared with those of either the Assembly of Saints or the Rump, and were much more in tune with the traditional arrangements under the old monarchy—exercised, however, under Independent supremacy. For Cromwell, "the great Independent", who claimed that once the Assembly of Saints had surrendered its power to him (this had been engineered by Lambert's followers in December 1653), his power was "as boundless and unlimited as before", now accepted the post of Lord Protector offered to him by the Council of Officers. He and his Council of State began promulgating ordinances which, according to "The Instrument", had the force of law until a new parliament was called. This new balanced constitution, it was hoped, would not only promote smooth government and put the Commonwealth upon a firm foundation, but win for the authority of Cromwell and his colleagues a wide national assent.

This hope proved entirely delusive when, on 3 September 1654 the first Protectorate Parliament met. To the new House of Commons thirty members were called from both conquered Scotland and conquered Ireland, who were in fact virtually the nominees of the army. Apart from them, it was a "free" parliament, chosen by free elections held mainly in the English counties (the number of boroughs was substantially reduced), and at least a hundred of its members had formerly been members of the Long Parliament. Such men were not at all likely to forgive or forget the affronts that they had once suffered at the hands of the army, which had first "purged" them and then expelled them. Nor were they likely to accept in a welcoming spirit the constitution that had suddenly been foisted upon the nation by the Army Grandees. Nor were they even likely to confirm, without considerable questioning, the ordinances imposed upon the nation by the Lord Protector and his Council.

In fact, the members of the first Protectorate Parliament at once made it clear that they proposed to regard themselves as a "constituent assembly" with the fullest authority to rewrite the "Instrument of Government". The out-and-out oligarchic Republicans, led by Cromwell's old enemy, Sir Arthur Haselrigg, soon won control of the leadership within the House, and outside it they were backed by an eclectic coalition of malcontents—Fifth Monarchy men, Levellers, left-wing Republicans, and even Royalists. This reaction confounded and confused the Protector's friends. The argument became furious : "It was disputed as if they had been in the schools, where each man had liberty to propose his own Utopia, and to frame a Commonwealth according to his own fancy, as if we had been in *republica constituenda* and not in *republica constituta*." So wrote a candid M.P. On 12 September Cromwell decided to affirm his authority as Lord Protector by force. He maintained that the new constitution had received the explicit approval of a greater part of the nation, while the members of parliament called under "The Instrument" had already promised by indentures signed on their behalf when they were elected to accept the government "by a single person and by parliament". He also emphasized that it was fundamental to this new constitution that parliaments should not be perpetual, that liberty of conscience should be upheld, and that control of the armed forces should be shared between the executive and parliament.

Although it is fashionable nowadays to assert that Oliver

Cromwell was neither a political thinker nor an imaginative statesman, it is fair to note, as Dr. Samuel Gardiner observed many years ago, that these "four fundamentals" of his have since been accepted by the British people as part of their unwritten constitution.

Cromwell demanded that if the members of parliament wished to continue sitting, they should specifically consent to these fundamentals of government. About three hundred members, many of them acknowledging the logic of the argument about their indentures, signed a recognition of the Protectoral Government and resumed the session. But this made little difference to the behaviour of the House. New leaders took the place of the old Republican stalwarts, who retired in protest and, as subsequent votes showed, the House was almost equally divided be-between a Court and a country party. The country party was determined that on no account would they permit the Protector to exercise any more than the formal powers which, after the first civil war broke out, had been offered by Cromwell himself and his friends to King Charles I. In fact, this party contended not for co-ordinate or balanced government but for the open supremacy of a single-chamber parliament. Cromwell, reared in the Elizabethan tradition of a "balanced constitution", regarded this simply as another name for "arbitrary government". Thus the old quarrel between King Charles I and the Long Parliament was resumed under a new guise, and the Puritans had fallen out among themselves.

Cromwell managed to maintain his patience with his first House of Commons until, according to a narrow interpretation of the letter of the "Instrument of Government", he had the right to dissolve it. During the late autumn of 1654 the attitude of the House hardened against the Lord Protector. It refused to consult him, except over one point, in its revision of the "Instrument", and it told him point-blank that he must give way to everything that it desired. In particular, it wanted to reduce the size of the army below what the Lord Protector believed to be a safety level and to deprive him of any control over the militia. On the whole, Cromwell behaved himself with dignity and restraint up to the last moment, but his officers were less taciturn and tactful than he was; and a proposal put forward in the House that he should be asked to become a hereditary monarch was foolish, ill-timed, and provocative. A meeting of the Army Council to swear loyalty to him also irritated the House; the tension between the executive and the legislature reached such a pitch of fury that the Royalists were encouraged to plot a rising. Finally, the House's grudging attitude towards toleration upset Cromwell, who always thought religious liberty more important than political liberty. So he dissolved parliament as soon as he could.

In his speech of dissolution, Cromwell accused the members of multiplying "dissettlement and division, discontent and dissatisfaction", together with real "dangers to the whole", of encouraging the Cavaliers and the Levellers (now negotiating an alliance with each other), of putting the army into a "distemper", of betraying the sacred cause of freedom of conscience. He denied that he himself had any personal ambitions in maintaining his office as Protector, and wrote that he desired "not to keep it an hour longer than I may preserve England in its just rights and may protect the people of God" in the just liberty of their conscience.

Such was the sad end, in reality, if not in Cromwell's own mind, to the experiment begun just over a year earlier in a balanced constitutional government. "Circumstances," wrote John Buchan with Scottish severity, "had forced him to assert a divine right to rule as stiff as any claim of Charles, and to dismiss the wishes of the governed in government with all the arrogance of Strafford." Likewise, Thomas Carlyle remarked : "By an arithmetical count of heads in England, the Lord Protector may surmise he had lost his Enterprise." Professor Trevor-Roper added : "He dissolved prematurely what was to have been his ideal parliament."

Nevertheless, it is a mistake to suppose that Oliver Cromwell had betrayed the revolution, at least the revolution for which he himself had taken up the sword. He still tried to adhere to the letter of the "Instrument of

Government"; he accepted the view of the Commons that his office must not be hereditary, that the army should be reduced, and taxation along with it. But he thought that a disinterested administration was now best suited to guide the fortunes of the nation, secure the religious fruits of the revolution, and strengthen the position of Britain as a power in the world.

Immediately parliament was dissolved, the insurrection forecast by Cromwell in his closing speech broke out. Both Royalists and Levellers were implicated, though they do not seem to have acted in concert. When it was suppressed, as it was without much difficulty, Cromwell was left with the problem how to maintain security at home and fight a now imminent war against Spain with a smaller military establishment. It is said that the idea of raising a horse militia for policing purposes was again owed by him to the fertile mind of Major-General John Lambert. By the end of 1655, this horse militia was raised at a cost of about £80,000 a year, which was to be paid for by a capital levy imposed upon all known Royalists in the country. It was argued that, strictly, such a levy was a breach of the Act of Oblivion of 1652; but it was plausibly defended on the ground that the Royalists were chiefly responsible for the rising which necessitated the introduction of the new security system. England and Wales were divided into eleven administrative districts, and Cromwell appointed his most trusted officers, headed by Lambert, by his son-in-law, Fleetwood, and by his brother-in-law, John Desborough, all with the local rank of major-general, to maintain law and order, to reinforce the authority of the local governments (since the civil war, local administration was in the hands of County Committees), and to raise the new tax on Royalists which was known as the "decimation" (because it was levied at the rate of ten per cent. upon their real property). An additional duty was also laid upon these major-generals, which was to stimulate virtue and discourage vice, a large order which embraced the prevention of blasphemy, drunkenness, and swearing.

It is not to be supposed that Cromwell himself regarded

the introduction of the major-generals—which was more or less an open military government—as a permanent part of the Puritan constitutional settlement. It was a security system imposed in an emergency, and so obviously contrary to the traditions of the nation (which had, after all, never known a standing army) as to be impracticable as a long-term solution to the problems of government. When the Spanish war began and the costs of government rose, the major-generals themselves pressed Cromwell to call a new parliament; he was not bound, according to the "Instrument", by which he still claimed to govern, to call another parliament until 1658, but he was entitled to call one to sit for three months in a national emergency. The emergency was the war. So Cromwell and his Council of State aimed to fashion a friendly House of Commons that would accept the existing Protectoral Government and vote him more money for the armed forces. Again the wheel had turned almost full circle and Cromwell appeared to be facing much the same problems as King Charles I.

This time the Protectoral Government was determined that the new House of Commons should be co-operative. Great efforts were reported in the constituencies, and during the régime of the major-generals many borough charters were altered with the aim of providing safe supporters for the Protector. The Council of State took advantage of a somewhat dubious interpretation of a clause in the "Instrument of Government" to examine the returns and to exclude ninety-nine of the members elected; others withdrew in protest at this high-handed conduct, so that in the event only about two hundred members attended the sittings of the new House. Of these, about a hundred were officials, army officers, and Cromwell's own relations. In the circumstances it was hardly surprising that Cromwell's personal position was confirmed, the war against Spain was approved, and a grant of money voted for its continuation.

On the other hand, in spite of the "purge", the House of Commons was soon to exhibit a now customary independence and, what was more significant, the Cromwellians in it were split among themselves. In the first place, after acrimonious debates, the House refused to approve or continue the system of government through local major-generals. On 29 January 1657, a new "Militia Bill" was defeated by 124 votes to 88. On the very next day the government was consoled for this setback by a vote of £400,000 towards the cost of the Spanish war and the proposal was put forward that Oliver Cromwell himself should be given the Crown.

The object of those who advocated this scheme for revising the Protectoral constitution in a monarchical sense was to disavow militarism or military government, and substitute for it a constitution upon a more traditional pattern that would fit the existing legal system of the country. Before the House had met, considerable doubt had been cast upon the lawfulness of the existing constitution, particularly by judges of the High Court. After all, this "Instrument of Government" had never been approved by anybody except the Council of Officers, and it had in effect been repudiated by the first Protectorate Parliament. The advocates of monarchy fancied that they might be able to reconcile Oliver Cromwell to a free parliament and a genuinely balanced constitution by offering him hereditary monarchy in his family : he was to be a kind of King Henry VII, the Cromwells replacing the Stuarts as the Tudors had replaced the Plantagenets. A new House of Lords—or at any rate a new Upper Chamber—was also to be created. Moreover, the powers of parliament were to be strengthened at the expense of those of the Council of State, and parliament was again given control over its own elections, with the added security that none of its members might be arbitrarily excluded by the executive. A further check upon the Protector was that a modest fixed revenue was to be written into the new constitution, while the method of its collection was to be settled solely by parliament.

Thus the House of Commons, while it was to be invited to restore something like the ancient constitution, was at the same time offered the chance of enhancing its own position and restricting that of the Crown in a way which neither the Tudors nor the Stuarts would have accepted.

In return for the bait of the Crown, Cromwell was being asked to break with the army. Opposition to this scheme, put forward mainly by lawyers and by ex-monarchists, naturally came from Cromwell's generals, especially John Lambert, Charles Fleetwood, and John Desborough. Cromwell himself admitted frankly that he was attracted by the proposals, for two reasons : first, he was tempted by the argument that his government would henceforward be put on a durable legal basis that could not be questioned either in parliament or in the courts, and thus the Puritan Revolution would at last have attained stability and respectability; secondly, he believed that if he were given the title of King he could acquire those powers of clemency and reprieve which had always been associated with the institution of monarchy, and be able to protect honest Christians from persecution. As we have seen, he had already been perturbed by an intolerant streak disclosed by members of the first Protectorate Parliament. The second parliament had equally shown itself intolerant by devoting a great deal of its time to planning horrific punishments for a crazy Quaker. But the Protector was hamstrung by his own past and his own following. Republican convictions had always burned most brightly among the Independents, and were now an almost passionate faith among many of the Puritan preachers. Moreover, his power still rested upon the loyalty of the army, where not only were most of the critics of a monarchical system, but where Levelling notions still lingered. Cromwell may have been no political thinker or at best an eclectic one, but he was no fool. He was aware of all the conflicting forces and parties that lapped around him. Paper constitutions might be persuasive, but they needed to be made workable by practical men and not by theorists. Experience had taught Cromwell that a settled government in the Commonwealth depended ultimately upon the power of the sword. To abandon and alienate his old friends was to invite mutiny, revolt, and anarchy. So, in the end, he decided to refuse the Crown, though he was willing to accept a new two-chamber constitution topped off with the added right to name his own successor as Lord Protector.

Did Cromwell, then, become the prisoner of the army, the victim of a monster he had created? The trouble was that by yielding to its wishes in regard to the Crown, he offended his latest supporters—"the new Cromwellians"—without reconciling his old ones. Like every other executive statesman—for example, King William III, Queen Anne, and some of the great presidents of the United States of America—he wanted to rule his country *above* party, but yet he found he could not do so; he could not, in fact, govern effectively without a party upon whose support he could rely. His heart, it may be said, was in the right place. "It is time," he is reported to have told a meeting of army officers on 7 March 1657, "to come to a settlement, and lay aside proceedings [military rule] so unacceptable to the nation." But in refusing the Crown, he had yielded to intense pressures; and in the end his new constitution gained him nothing except the gratifications of a dying dynast. For when in January 1658 this friendly parliament met once again, the excluded members had to be readmitted, in accordance with this new constitution known as "The Humble Petition and Advice", and his own supporters were first divided and then swamped, the leadership regained for the third time by his old enemy, Sir Arthur Haselrigg. The independent House of Commons of the sixteen-forties rose again like a phœnix from the ashes.

Thus it was that once more, as in 1654, the majority of the Commons settled down with relish to constitution-mongering and political sabotage. The creation of an Upper Chamber, or a revised House of Lords, furnished Haselrigg and his friends with a magnificent opportunity for mischief. For Haselrigg himself, a proud, morose man, had been appointed to the new second House by Cromwell, but firmly refused to go there, preferring to take the oath to be faithful to the Lord Protector's person : "I will murder no man", he said with defiant joy. After Cromwell had addressed both the Houses, the Commons demanded a report of his speech, and angrily questioned his right to treat both Houses upon an equal basis. Haselrigg's friend, Thomas Scot, spread himself into lengthy historical disquisition, reminding his audience, among other things, how the Lords had refused to join in the trial of King Charles I. In vain Cromwell pleaded with the members for political unity in the name of patriotism and religion, reminding them that the war against Spain had still to be won and that European Protestantism was under attack. Once again an opposition to the Lord Protector was formed within the House and agitators stirred themselves outside. This time Cromwell was under no constitutional obligation to keep the parliament in being for five months, and he allowed his temper to take hold of him. Only a fortnight after its first meeting, on 20 January 1658, he dissolved his second Protectorate Parliament.

So collapsed the last of Cromwell's constitutional experiments, although not the last form of government to be tried during the Interregnum. Threatened with mutiny, treason, and anarchy, Oliver Cromwell had once more felt compelled to take drastic action. Historians, as is their wont, have distributed the blame for this failure in political harmony in various different ways. Some lay it squarely upon Cromwell himself, maintaining that his lack of tact, imagination, or patience had undermined an established parliamentary system. The latest view is that he was "a natural back-bencher" without any effective political following and was doomed to fail as a constructive statesman; while a "settlement" with or without monarchy was a mere mirage. Or, to put it differently, the only source of settlement was, as his own son Henry saw, Cromwell's own leadership and personality.

It is certainly much easier to analyse why the five or six different experiments in forms of government which were tried between the execution of King Charles I and the death of Oliver Cromwell nearly ten years later did not succeed, than to decide how they might have succeeded. It is extremely simple to indict the jealousies and rivalries of parties, the conservatism of an inarticulate people, or the restlessness of too articulate parliaments, or to point to a lack of clear and realistic political thought. But is it not a fact that there was far too much political thinking in mid-seventeenth-century England, ranging from the democratic idealism of the Levellers to the selfish oligarchism of Haselrigg, from the constructive ingenuities of John Lambert to the new monarchism of the ex-Royalist Cromwellians, while there was too little constructive give-and-take among the victorious Puritans? It is easy, too, to condemn Cromwell himself for his temporary flights into military dictatorship—though even when the major-generals ruled it never existed upon anything like the horrific scale that we ourselves have seen in many countries in modern times from Spain to Hungary.

To put it brutally, the reason for Cromwell's failure to establish a settled government, with or without the aid of parliaments, was not that he was too ruthless but that he was not ruthless enough. Who, for example, were to emerge from the French Revolution but first the Terrorists and then Napoleon Bonaparte before the Bourbons were recalled? How did the Russian Revolution reach stability, except by calculated terror? Hitler and other modern dictators, too, attained one-party government through revolutionary blood-baths. After the civil war was over, Cromwell aimed, understandably enough, at a balanced constitution, and though he purged his parliaments, he at least allowed them to sit and criticize him, and tried hard to come to terms with them. The historical critic cannot have it both ways. The paradoxical truth is that Cromwell failed to secure a peaceful and progressive government in an England that was confused and divided precisely because, unable to enlist military co-operation he yet refused to be either a king or a tyrant.

Chapter Eleven

The English People
and the Protectorate

THE life of ordinary men and women in seventeenth-century England must always have been hard. Most of them lived upon a mere margin of subsistence, in windowless cottages and insanitary tenements, with virtually no medical care or attention, often the victims of harsh laws and customs, designed for the benefit of their betters. Few of them can have known what the civil wars were about, why King and parliament had quarrelled, or what was the nature of the religious disputes that divided their masters. It has even been suggested that many of them did not go to church and conned their religion from the various badly printed Bibles that flooded the country, and from wandering preachers, who were self-taught or crazily inspired. Their recreation consisted of visits to the taverns—which were numerous—when they could be afforded (the price of beer was a halfpenny a quart); courting took place in lanes or alleyways; women who gave birth to illegitimate children received little mercy from the authorities; games of a crude sort were played, including football and skittles; but excitement would be aroused by such cruel sports as cock-fighting. Later pictures of a Merry England are largely imaginative. For the vast majority, existence upon earth was short, brutish and nasty.

The ordinary agricultural labourer might earn 8*d*. a day or a shilling, with his keep; the skilled craftsman 2*s*. a day. Corresponding to this was a rate of pay of 8*d*. a day and all found for the foot soldier, with three times as much for the cream of the army, the mounted troopers. A woman was lucky if she were paid 2*s*. 6*d*. a week, and the hours of labour lasted from five in the morning till sunset in the winter, or till about seven in the evening in the summer. As Puritanism grew more influential, restrictions upon Sunday amusements were imposed and enforced, and instead of Saints' Days, city apprentices were allowed to take a holiday on the second Tuesday of each month, when they usually got into mischief. It is likely that the civil wars, by drawing some 100,000 able-bodied men into the rival armies, created more work for the remainder, but as soon as the wars were over, the interruptions to business that they had caused and the return of ex-soldiers into the labour market contributed to an unemployment problem which seems to have been at about its worst at the time King Charles I was executed. Political uncertainty and foreign wars had also helped to bring about a temporary economic depression. The chief reason why the establishment of the Protectorate in 1654 was popular was because people in general hoped for domestic peace and a business revival after the ending of the Dutch war.

Gradually the economic situation mended. But while harvests were better and the price of wheat was reduced, money wages also fell for a time, and a large number of people remained unemployed. The methods of dealing with poverty and unemployment were severe. The administration of the poor laws had largely broken down during the civil wars. Both John Lilburne and Sir Matthew Hale, a judge who had been a Royalist, urged upon the authorities the need for something more in the way of relief than the mere levying of assessments by parishes to assist the aged and impotent; they wanted work to be provided by parish officers. On the whole, however, these questions were left to be solved locally. At quarter sessions, the Justices of the Peace might vote the distribution of cheap food to the poor, or the Justices of Assize might order a rate to be levied in areas smitten by plague or epidemic, but poverty and idleness were regarded as sinful in the Puritan scheme of life, and little of a positive character was achieved.

Soon after Cromwell became Protector, an ordinance was published allowing soldiers demobilized from his army to take up their trades again without fulfilling the apprenticeship laws, and legislation was passed to give relief to wounded soldiers. Dr. Margaret James wrote that while between the years 1645 and 1660 "Parliament seems to have been struggling to evolve a constructive and comprehensive system of relief and employment for the poor, yet the only measures which passed into law were those which had to do with the suppression of vagrants". In 1656 a committee was ordered to prepare a Bill to enable stocks to be raised to set the poor at work, but it never reached the statute book. In London a Corporation for the Poor, which had been set up in 1647, concentrated not very successfully upon suppressing beggars. In the counties the major-generals employed their new police force to lend aid to the local magistrates in coping with the "idle poor". The army was also called in at various times to try to maintain law and order upon the highways, where robbery was common. Several highwaymen were caught and punished. In general, Cromwell's government managed to maintain the English roads in fair condition, to supply regular postal services, and to keep the highways clear of thieves and beggars. Good intentions were not lacking in regard to social reform; the Puritans did not lack charity—Cromwell himself was both generous and compassionate—but the poor law policy of the Interregnum has been described as one of "harshness coupled with failure".

This much, however, should be said on the other side. Such evidence as we have indicates that the years between the ending of the Dutch war in the spring of 1654 and the death of Oliver Cromwell in the autumn of 1658 were ones of comparative prosperity, with good harvests, a developing foreign trade, and a fair level of real wages. In spite of the demobilization of part of the army, unemployment gradually diminished, and the navy, army, and horse militia upon which substantial sums of public money had been spent, must have helped to furnish employment. The Council of State did what it could to stimulate local authorities into assisting the poor in areas where unemployment was reported, and the Assize judges were quite as conscientious as they had been in the reign of King

Charles I in investigating social problems and proposing relief. Nor is there any reason to suppose that the "new gentry", who were responsible for the county administration, were either less hard working or less considerate than their predecessors. At the centre of government the Council of State, both before and after the Protectorate was set up, met every afternoon and covered a wide range of problems from running the wars to fixing the prices of food and drink, from appointing public officials to ordering the grass to be cut at Hampton Court. But its chief difficulty, as with the Lord Protector, was how to translate its good purposes into law, and then to obtain the enforcement of the law throughout the country.

As to domestic reform, the Protectorate Government concentrated chiefly upon the administration of the laws, education, manners, and the Church. In most of these matters it carried on from where the Long Parliament had left off. On the whole, the Rump Parliament was slow and relatively ineffective, while the Assembly of Saints had been quick and rash, if well meaning. The need for the reform of the law was a question about which Cromwell and his fellow soldiers felt strongly : for there was widespread conviction, expressed with animation in many pamphlets of the time, that the law was customarily subject to many unnecessary delays, that its administration favoured the wealthy, and that its penalties were too heavy. Lawyers were unpopular, and were condemned by the Levellers as being the "vermin of the Commonwealth". Cromwell himself once said that laws that made one man rich and many poor did not suit a Commonwealth, and that "to see men lose their lives for petty matters is a thing God will reckon".

A beginning had been made with an Act of 1650, which ordered that henceforward all proceedings in the law courts should be conducted in English and not in French or Latin, except in the case of the High Court of Admiralty, which was concerned with international litigation. The Rump also passed a resolution that parties to a dispute should get to trial at once and not be held up by complicated special pleadings. In 1652 it voted further that the High Court judges in Westminster Hall should only receive their salaries (fixed at £1,000 a year) and not demand as well fees, presents, and perquisites. But very little progress had been achieved with law reform when Cromwell returned from Worcester. Among his first actions when he became Lord Protector were to secure the appointment of first-class judges both in England and Ireland, regardless of their party affiliations, to pardon men condemned to death for minor offences, and to appoint a committee "to consider how the laws might be made plain and short, and less chargeable to the people".

A principal grievance of the time was the Court of Chancery. The old prerogative courts, like the Star Chamber, the High Commission, the Court of Wards and Liveries, as well as the Councils of Wales and of the North, and the criminal jurisdiction of the ecclesiastical courts, had been swept away on the first tide of the revolution; and while a High Court of Justice had been introduced to deal with the same kind of treasonable offences that had previously been the concern of the Star Chamber, the only other court now functioning which did not follow along the traditional lines of the Common Law, was the Chancery or Equity Court. Equity was not a definite system and Chancellors or Commissioners of the Great Seal were said to have enjoyed too much freedom both to extend their jurisdiction and to interfere with that of the Common Law Courts. John Selden said that equity was, in effect, the length of the Chancellor's foot, and it was claimed that over 20,000 cases were pending in the Court, some of them for a period of up to thirty years, thus "bleeding the people". The Assembly of Saints had wanted to abolish the Court out of hand, but that would only have worsened the chaos.

Cromwell and his Council of State therefore exerted what pressure they could on the leading lawyers of the day to reform Chancery procedure. An ordinance was drafted and passed in August 1654, with the aim both of reducing its delays and its costs. "The principle upon which the ordinance was framed," wrote Sir William Holdsworth, "was a thorough distrust of the persons who would have to enforce it." No wonder that two of the three Commissioners of the Great Seal refused to work it and preferred to resign. Cromwell bore them no animosity. The Master of the Rolls is said to have vowed that he would be hanged at Rolls Gate before he would execute the ordinance. Such weighty opposition ruined the new measure and, after an experimental period of three years, it had to be dropped. Cromwell also insisted that only murder, treason, and rebellion should be deemed crimes worthy of capital punishment, and in fact during his Protectorate this principle seems to have been accepted. But the absorption of Cromwell's parliaments in constitutional squabbles and the steady resistance of the most influential lawyers to any radical reforms prevented as much being accomplished as the Lord Protector wished. The criminal code was not materially lightened until the nineteenth century.

The reform of manners went forward more rapidly, for it was in tune with the spirit of the times. Some of the former jurisdiction of the ecclesiastical courts, such as that relating to marriages and wills, was shifted to civil courts. Civil marriage, accompanied by the necessary procedure of registration, was instituted by the Assembly of Saints, but, in spite of the advocacy of John Milton, no opening was allowed for divorce, which virtually required a private Act of Parliament. An Act making adultery a capital offence was passed in May 1650, but it became a dead letter. The Assize Courts and Quarter Sessions, however, interested themselves in fornication, and Cromwell's major-generals were called upon to uphold the strict sexual morality of the Puritans. A Bill prohibiting women from painting their faces and wearing patches or immodest dresses surprisingly never became law, but various attempts were made to enforce or supplement the sumptuary laws of the Middle Ages which aimed at preventing extravagances or indecencies in clothing and personal adornment. Swearing was punishable by a scale of fines. It cost a duke thirty shillings and a gentleman 6s. 8d. Excessive drinking was also frowned upon. The Justices of the Peace were urged to suppress unlicensed ale-houses and some of the major-generals showed a positive delight in closing down out-of-the-way taverns, nominally at any rate for reasons of national security. For the same reasons a number of horse-races were prohibited in 1655 and 1656. It is likely that inns and race meetings were in fact centres of conspiracy against the government (it is known that John Wildman, the Leveller leader, made good use of them). Cromwell himself had no objection in principle to good citizens enjoying their glass of ale and humane sports. He was aware in his heart that one could not reform manners or morals by mere prohibitions, and he thought it absurd that all wine should be kept out of a country "lest men should be drunk". Indeed, he himself enjoyed a glass of wine and a pipe.

It was a golden age for education. Schools and universities, like every other side of public life, had been dislocated by the civil war. But the Acts abolishing bishops and deans and confiscating Church properties did not mean the dissolution of schools hitherto largely paid for out of ecclesiastical endowments. For example, Westminster School, which belonged to the Dean and Chapter of Westminster Abbey, was given a new corporate body to govern it, and its revenues were vested in trustees. Many new free schools were established—sixty of them in Wales alone—and schoolmasters were selected and approved by a so-called "Committee for Plundered Ministers". A few schoolmasters were inevitably dismissed because of their Royalist sympathies, but some of them at least were allowed to set up on their own or to teach in private schools. The warden of Winchester, the headmaster of Westminster, and the headmaster of King's School, Canterbury, were all left in possession, although accused of Royalism, and other headmasters hastened to conform. An Act "for providing ministers and other pious uses", passed in 1651, named trustees who were empowered to give grants to increase schoolmasters' salaries.

The universities also flourished after the end of the civil wars. Cromwell had a long-standing local interest in Cambridge and accepted the Chancellorship of Oxford. Royalist heads of colleges were driven out, and the Puritan influx tended to encourage discipline and application in the universities and to awaken them from lethargy and a traditional curriculum. A movement was set on foot to found a new university in the north of England to instil "prudent and religious education", and in 1657 Cromwell was personally responsible for establishing a college at Durham, which was partly paid for out of the unsold revenues of the Dean and Chapter of the Cathedral. Cromwell also thought of founding a new college at Oxford to be named St. Mary's Hall, where "a general synopsis of the true reformed Protestant Christian religions professed in the Commonwealth" should be drawn up. The idea of having a "glorious university" in London was also conceived. In general, this was a period of lively activity in education. Nothing is more wrong than to suppose that the age of Cromwell and Milton was an intellectual trough. The London of the sixteen-fifties was a centre of original philosophic and scientific thought.

This liveliness of thought, exemplified in writers as various as the philosophers Hobbes and Harrington, the poets Milton and Marvell, and the educationist John Dury, the political theorists William Walwyn and Gerrard Winstanley—to name only a few—owed much to the climate of the times. The Church of England, it is true, had already by King Charles I's reign begun to become a religious society which permitted comprehensive points of view, and had nurtured such theologians as Hooker, Andrewes, Donne, Chillingworth, and Jeremy Taylor; but the overthrow of its hierarchy by the Puritans had given an even keener stimulus to liberty of thought. At first it looked as if one system of all-embracing ecclesiastical government would merely give way to another. The need for an Anglo-Scottish alliance to defeat the King which had been accepted by John Pym, had appeared to demand the price of a Presbyterian Church in both countries. But the Long Parliament kept an extremely firm hand upon the deliberations of the Assembly of Divines that was set up in 1643 to work out a programme for an entirely new Church. Though the Assembly laboured for six years or more, it never succeeded in constructing this new edifice, which might have been more intolerant than the old. The reason was that the Independents and Erastians, both in the Assembly and in the Commons, were determined that they would never allow the religious organization of the nation to be dictated to them by Scottish theologians. While in theory the English Commonwealth Government was committed when it took over in 1649 to a Presbyterian Church—with some toleration outside it for dissenting sects—in fact confusion reigned supreme; as Dr. W. A. Shaw observed : "All attempts at a religious settlement subsequent to 1649 took the form of such a definition of toleration as would secure the liberty of individual men and congregations on the one hand and as would guard the State against the dangers of Popery and blasphemy on the other."

It was Oliver Cromwell's main contribution to English history, on which he prided himself, that he was strong enough to maintain religious freedom in the face of the intolerant attitude displayed by the majority in the Interregnum parliaments. We have seen how Cromwell's chaplain, Dr. John Owen, who later became Vice-Chancellor of Oxford University, put forward a scheme for religious toleration which was rejected by the Assembly of Saints in 1653. "The Instrument of Government" laid down in three of its clauses that "the Christian religion, as contained in the Scriptures, be held forth and recommended as the public profession of these nations"; but that "to the public profession held forth none shall be compelled by penalties or otherwise"; and that "of such as profess faith in God by Jesus Christ" none should be restrained so long as they did not disturb the public peace. That liberty, however, did not extend to "Popery and Prelacy". Arrangements were to be made to provide teachers able to instruct the people in "sound doctrine"; but until that had been done, the existing method of paying ministers by tithes was to be continued.

"The Instrument", in fact, merely outlined broad and undefined conditions for the future religious policy of the country. What was "sound doctrine"? Who were to be included among those who "professed faith by Jesus Christ"? Did they include, for example, Unitarians? How was a new system for the payment of ministers to be worked out? Cromwell's own idea of a comprehensive Church was disclosed by his immediate adoption of Owen's plan, and the appointment of Triers to examine the qualifications of candidates for livings and Ejectors to remove scandalous or inefficient ministers. But an attempt by parliament to set up yet another assembly of divines to frame a public profession of Christianity or to explain what was meant by "faith in Jesus Christ" soon collapsed. Nor did the appointment of committees to pay augmentations to ministers' stipends (the same committees that concerned themselves with schoolmasters) resolve the tricky question of tithes or the general problems of Church endowment. Cromwell's two parliaments showed themselves bigoted, and were far from ready to place a liberal interpretation upon the meaning of the Christian faith. The "Humble Petition and Advice" of 1657 added little to the religious clauses embodied in the "Instrument of Government". This paper constitution also professed willingness to permit toleration of Christians outside the Church, and demanded that a "confession of faith" should be agreed between the Lord Protector and parliament; but again it looked to the future; and the fierce behaviour of the House of Commons towards the unfortunate Quaker, James Naylor, ill accorded with a tolerant outlook. In fact, the religious policy of the Protectorate was largely settled by administrative action; that is to say, by Cromwell himself.

Some historians have described the Protectorate as a time of spiritual anarchy, others as one of sheer confusion. But that is scarcely fair. A clear and firm conception of how religion should be organized existed in Cromwell's mind. He was prepared to allow each congregation to appoint or approve its own ministers, subject to a few overriding qualifications of worth, to supplement existing benefices upon the lines later pursued in Queen Anne's Bounty, to allow new churches or chapels to be formed, and even to tolerate the holding of services according to the old Anglican rites or the still older Roman Catholic rites in private houses, so long as such services did not lead to a breach of the peace or afford covers for plotting against the national security. He permitted the Jews to return and

settle in England and to have their own synagogue and
cemetery in London. Above all, he insisted that no man
should be punished for his private thoughts or beliefs.
Secure in his own personal faith, he felt no urge to force
his own beliefs upon others. Hard as it may be for the
modern mind to appreciate, his genuinely tolerant outlook
did not stem from indifference but from its opposite. He
preferred liberty of conscience to intellectual tidiness; he
did not believe that men could be compelled to faith by
the sword. Thus Congregationalism, Presbyterianism,
Baptism, and the Society of Friends all look back to the
Interregnum as a time of growth; they become sufficiently
rooted so that the traditions of Nonconformity or Dissent
have shaped British political and social history ever since.

How far this liberal attitude of mind extended to
economic affairs during the Protectorate is difficult to
assess. The medieval approach of paternalism was breaking down, but old habits died hard. Thus the structure of
wage and price fixing, the prescription of standards of
work, the upholding of craft guilds and apprenticeship
regulations continued. There was some democratization of
the guilds; industrial and commercial monopolies met
with public criticism. The problem was, as always, to distinguish between justifiable rules and mere restraints upon
trade. To determine what was an economic monopoly and
what was a reasonable patent, the government looked for
legal advice. Equally, while there was opposition in Puritan circles to the maintenance of monopolies in commerce,
it was recognized that its regulation was essential. For instance, though for a time the Protector threw open the
East Indian trade, the old company reasonably argued
that it could not afford to pay for forts and trading posts
in India unless it was given the right to charge for the
admission of merchants who made use of them. Thus,
upon the advice of his Council of State, Cromwell granted
a new charter to the old joint stock company in 1657. The
Merchant Adventurers, the Levant Company, and the
Greenland Company were also at length upheld in their
privileges. Nevertheless, a large number of "interlopers"
managed to earn a living from foreign trade, and the

nearer countries, such as France, Portugal, and the Scandinavian group, with which business was done, were virtually left open to all-comers. The power of the English navy and its exploits in the Mediterranean proved advantageous to English commerce, and broadly the Interregnum seems to have been an era of freer and prospering trade.

This prosperity was reflected in the customs and excise returns on which the national finances were based. The cost of waging the civil wars had required the invention of new forms of taxation, of which the most prominent were the excise and the monthly assessments. The excise was a tax on consumption, imitated from abroad and first introduced in 1643. The monthly assessments were taxes on property apportioned between the counties and there levied at fixed rates upon rents and also upon personal property. In practice, the excise took the place of the old feudal dues and the assessments of the medieval subsidies, both of which had grown out of date and yielded comparatively little. Naturally these new taxes were unpopular, just as ship money had been; but they were efficient, and, together with the customs, were the main sources from which the army and navy were paid. When the civil wars ended, the expenditure of the government did not materially fall, partly because of the expense of garrisoning Ireland and Scotland, partly because the army was still needed for security, and partly because of the wars that were waged against the Dutch and the Spaniards. When, under pressure from his first Protectorate Parliament, Cromwell reduced the size of the army and the rate of the monthly assessments, he was still left with a security problem, which was temporarily resolved by the institution of the major-generals and the "decimation" of the Royalists.

Up to the beginning of the Protectorate, the Long Parliament had been able to sustain a high level of public expenditure by means of selling off the King's properties and the properties of the Church, and by fining Royalists who were obliged to compound for their estates. A complicated committee system dealt piecemeal with these varied sources of revenue. Most of them were exhausted when

Cromwell became Protector. His government gradually wound up the committees and put the administration of public finance upon a more satisfactory basis. The Exchequer course was restored, and all tax revenues were paid into one Treasury with a proper system of audit and control. The monthly assessments alone were not directly controlled by the Exchequer, partly because as a novel tax it did not fit into the old system, but chiefly no doubt because the commander-in-chief wished to keep the fund out of which the army was paid, in the hands of the Treasurers at War.

The financial changes of the Interregnum had considerable social significance. The vast sales of lands, not merely those belonging to the Church and King but also to Royalists, who were compelled to part with some of their properties to pay their fines or through confiscation, caused values to depreciate and enabled enterprising speculators, including merchants, financiers, army officers, and other officials, to make money, sometimes by selling back land to the very Royalists from whom it was confiscated. Secondly, the abolition of outmoded feudal dues and incidents, such as those that King Charles I's ministers had exploited during the so-called "eleven years' tyranny", and the introduction of the excise, which was subject to parliamentary control, strengthened the power of the Commons over the Crown when the Restoration came. On the other hand, these new taxes and the accumulation of public debts, relatively heavy for a time when funding was not invented, discontented both the smaller gentry and the shopkeeping classes, and though that discontent was not of major importance so long as Oliver Cromwell himself ruled, it contributed to a general sense of dissatisfaction which helped the recall of the Stuarts after he was dead.

Chapter Twelve

The English Commonwealth
and the World

FOUR principal aims guided Cromwell's foreign policy as Protector: to maintain and spread the Protestant religion; to preserve and expand English trade; to prevent the restoration of the Stuarts to the English throne by foreign aid; and to enhance the prestige of the Commonwealth.

The first thing he did was to make peace with the Dutch. Cromwell had always disliked this war against a sister Protestant Republic, and had no wish to pursue it to unconditional surrender. Indeed, what he had in mind was to follow up the idea originally mooted by the envoys of the Rump Parliament—that of promoting an intimate political alliance between the two countries. One suggestion he put forward was that "both sides should admit in their governments two or three lords", that is to say, two or three Dutchmen were to join the English Council of State and two or three Englishmen allowed into the Dutch government. The Dutch were not prepared for any such revolutionary political federation, but their ambassadors soon realized that Cromwell was eager for peace. Still, for the Dutch the terms they accepted were pretty onerous; they amounted to a full confession of defeat. Not only did the Dutch admit the supremacy of the English flag in English seas, but they promised to pay reparations. In addition to abandoning the Royalist cause and expelling the Royalist exiles from their country, a secret promise was given to exclude the Prince of Orange, son of an English princess, from all commands. That treaty, concluded in April 1654, was buttressed by another treaty with Denmark, whereby the Baltic Sound was reopened to English ships and the same dues exacted from them as from the Dutch merchantmen. Later in the year a commercial treaty was arranged with Sweden and another with Portugal, by which her King promised to pay reparations for losses suffered by English merchants (when earlier help had been given to Prince Rupert's Royalist fleet), to guarantee freedom to English merchants and sailors from the Inquisition, and to afford full liberty for trade with the Portuguese colonies. All these treaties, therefore, won advantages for English commerce, upheld the Protestant interest, and provided guarantees against Royalist invasions. France hastened to offer recognition of the Protectorate Government, and King Charles II was obliged to seek refuge in Cologne.

Thus in addressing his first parliament, Cromwell was able to speak of "an honourable peace", of improved prospects for trade, of promising negotiations with France; and he could declare : "There is not a nation in Europe but they are very willing to ask a good understanding of you."

The main problem that now confronted Cromwell and his Council of State, whose advice he was required by the "Instrument of Government" to take upon questions of foreign policy, was whether he should conclude an offensive alliance with either of his Catholic neighbours, France and Spain. These two kingdoms were at war, and the position was complicated by the fact that one of the best French generals, the Prince de Condé, was in rebellion against the French Regency effectively directed by Cardinal Mazarin, the astute Italian who was the lover of the Queen Mother—and was allied with Spain. The ambassadors of Mazarin, Condé, and the Spanish King Philip IV, all sought to hire Cromwell's famous soldiers. Even before Cromwell became Protector, suggestions had come from France that the port of Dunkirk, which had belonged to the Spanish empire but had been temporarily captured by the French, might be surrendered to the English in return for their military assistance. The Spaniards offered the port of Calais, if it could be won from the French, and Condé offered La Rochelle. All these were big temptations.

Other factors influenced the important decision that now had to be taken. One of these was what was called "the Protestant interest". Some of the French Protestants or Huguenots were fighting for Condé, and he appealed strongly for help on their behalf. It was even said that he had been ready to declare himself a Protestant. Equally it would have been a splendid feather in the Lord Protector's cap if he could have exacted from the Spanish grandees freedom of worship for English Protestant traders throughout the Spanish dominions. Or, again, he might have obliged Cardinal Mazarin to give public guarantees of liberty of conscience for the French Protestants as the price of a military alliance. Another consideration was finance. The Dutch war had been costly and the capital resources of the Commonwealth were exhausted. The army was still largely occupied in security duties, and it was the navy that needed employment. It was also argued that peace was necessary in order to restore commercial and industrial prosperity, that it was wiser to allow English merchants to benefit from the commercial treaties just concluded and to trade freely with both France and Spain than to run the risk of reprisals from one side or the other.

So the negotiations of 1654 and 1655 were prolonged and complicated, and the English Council of State was torn in mind over what was the best policy. Some of its members advocated war with France, others war with Spain, and a few were neutral. The anti-French party argued that revenge must be taken upon the French pirates operating from ports like St. Malo, that the Huguenots must not be allowed to "barter themselves away", and that it was a mistake to sacrifice a profitable trade with Spain, particularly in the export of cloth, for the mirage of captured treasure. The anti-Spanish party looked back to the precedents of Queen Elizabeth's reign, and thought it would be much easier to acquire a port in the Spanish Netherlands with French assistance than to conquer a French port with Spanish aid; it was also thought more

feasible to give help to the French Huguenots by diplomatic pressure than by war. Moreover, Cromwell's government had sent spies into the Protestant areas of France,
who reported that they showed little enthusiasm for rising
against the Bourbon monarchy. In the end, the Spanish
ambassador was asked outright if English merchants could
be given freedom to trade in the West Indies and to practice their religion without danger from the Inquisition,
and the blunt reply came that this was to ask for the King
his master's "two eyes".

So it was in reality the middle or neutral party that won
the decision in the argument over foreign policy in the
Council of State. It may be doubted if Cromwell himself
ever nursed any serious intentions of concluding a Spanish
alliance, but by flirting with Spain he wanted to induce
Cardinal Mazarin to make open concessions and especially
to give pledges to the Huguenots. If that was the aim, he
was disappointed. And in the autumn of 1654, it was
decided to find work for the navy. Two expeditions were
planned : one was to set sail for the West Indies to revenge
itself upon the Spaniards for the exclusion of English trade
there by seizing and fortifying one of the bigger Spanish
islands and using it as a stepping-stone towards the coveted
gold-mines of South America or as a base from which
Spanish treasure ships might be attacked. The commanders of the expedition were expected to regard themselves
as Protestant missionaries as well as commercial travellers
and pupils of Ralegh and Drake. The other expedition,
under the command of General Robert Blake, was destined
for the Mediterranean, to redeem English captives and
enforce respect for the English flag in North Africa. Both
commanders were instructed to continue reprisals against
French privateers. Thus, in effect, undeclared naval war
was to be intensified against both France and Spain. Such
a provocative and dangerous policy was more likely to lead
to a European struggle than to peace.

When the news of these expeditions leaked out, the
French under the wily Mazarin turned the other cheek;
but the Spaniards did not. Negotiations for a French
treaty still continued. King Louis XIV reaffirmed the

Edict of Nantes, which had been designed to protect the Huguenots, and private assurances about their welfare were conveyed to Whitehall. When, in 1655, a Protestant sect known as the Vaudois, who dwelt in the Alpine valleys, were attacked by troops of the Roman Catholic Regent of Savoy, Cromwell, acting his self-chosen part of protector of the Protestants, demanded French intervention in Savoy as a price of his signing the treaty. He also contemplated bringing Blake's fleet to bear down upon the south coast of France. Mazarin yielded and obliged the Duke of Savoy, as a client ruler, to sign a treaty with the Vaudois, and the first Anglo-French treaty was finally concluded in October 1655. On the same day as that on which the treaty was signed, the Spanish ambassador left London as a protest at the West Indies expedition, and a broader and more direct war between England and Spain became a certainty.

The first treaty signed with the French during the Protectorate was only a commercial one, at any rate on paper, but Cromwell was promised separately that the leading Royalists, apart from the widow of King Charles I, should be expelled from France, while on the English side the negotiators made it clear that a closer alliance was likely to follow. With the French alliance, in fact, there opened a period of anti-Habsburg diplomacy. Cromwell played with the idea of heading a coalition, not only against the Spanish but also against the Austrian Habsburgs, and of bringing into it the Dutch, the Danes, the Swedes, and even the Catholics of Portugal, who had only recently broken away from Spain. Might not the French monarchy's concessions to the Huguenots and Mazarin's intervention on behalf of the Vaudois of Savoy constitute a very happy precedent for a foreign policy attuned to the Protestant interest? And while Protestantism was being made safe in Europe, the far-flung men-of-war of the English Commonwealth might help to establish new colonies in Spanish America under Protestant influence.

Such, broadly, were the grandiose schemes of Oliver Cromwell, though it is doubtful if he would have formulated them exactly in that way. For, as we can read in his opening speech to his second parliament, he maintained that his foreign policy was not aggressive but defensive. To him the Spaniards were the "natural enemy" of the English people, and their design was "the empire of the whole Christian world, if not more". An English envoy had been murdered in Madrid, the blood of English traders had been shed in the West Indies, the Royalists had been stirred up and "Spaniolized". Cromwell's government did not differ from any other in modern history in affirming with its hand on its heart that it was not the aggressor in the coming war; but it was difficult to laugh off the elaborately planned expedition against the West Indies, which was both provocative and unsuccessful.

To compensate for their failure to acquire one of the larger and wealthier Spanish West Indian islands—they had been ignominiously repulsed from San Domingo—the commanders of the expedition occupied the then almost barren island of Jamaica in May 1655, which thus became the first colony in British history to be gained by deliberate government action. When Cromwell heard the news in July he was gravely disappointed, and shut himself up in his room, brooding over what he conceived to be a major disaster and a punishment from on high. His over-ambitious policy of colonizing South America or exacting a toll on its riches had proved impracticable. Not even the dispatch of the disgraced commanders to the Tower of London could conceal from the public the fact that this failure was to be attributed largely to the Lord Protector himself. However, later he recovered his spirits : he and his Council of State successfully exerted themselves to keep Jamaica in British hands, and convert it into a prosperous outpost of the British Commonwealth, as it has been ever since.

Whatever the motives for the colonization of Jamaica, it was a unique experiment in being the first oversea possession to be conquered by a British expeditionary force sent out by the home government. Throughout the seventeenth and indeed even in the eighteenth century, the British West Indian colonies were regarded as precious and promising. Barbados and the Leeward Islands, al-

ready settled by private companies of adventurers, were
expected to yield rich returns in cotton and tobacco. Barbados in fact was to produce a wealthy planter aristocracy,
made fabulously rich by the sugar plantations. Earlier an
abortive scheme for colonizing Providence Island had received the backing of many eminent Puritans, including
John Pym. This, like some of the settlements in New
England, was a forerunner of the English Puritan colonial
impulse. In a sense, Cromwell was the heir to these
schemes of his Puritan friends. To begin with, as was
originally expected, buccaneering was the most paying industry in Jamaica; later it was to become famous for sugar
and rum. Cromwell tried to persuade some of the settlers
in New England to transfer themselves to Jamaica; he saw
to it that it was adequately victualled and garrisoned, and
he appointed experienced men as governors. A West Indian committee was set up in London to look after it and
the other British possessions in the Caribbean.

But in those times of slow and uncertain communications, English settlers across the Atlantic were largely their
own masters. When the civil wars were in progress a
number of Royalists went to Virginia (first colonized in
1607) and to Barbados (colonized in 1625). An Act of Parliament of 1650 forbade all commercial intercourse with
these two colonies, as well as with Antigua and Bermuda,
which had also declared their Royalist sympathies. In the
following year, Sir George Ayscue was dispatched with a
fleet to enforce obedience to the Commonwealth and captured several Dutch ships trading there. In the same year
the Navigation Act had been passed, which confined all
trade with the plantations to English vessels. The New
England colonies, on the other hand, were not Royalist,
and while in 1643 some of them formed themselves into a
federation for self-protection, they acknowledged the
authority of the English Commonwealth and indeed became the outposts of the new Puritanism.

Thus, by the time that Cromwell became Lord Protector, the colonies all acknowledged the new English government, some of them more reluctantly than others. But
none of them cared for the protectionist policy of the

Navigation Acts, and Dutch ships still managed to trade with them in spite of such restrictions. Soon the Council of State realized that these distant territories could not be provisioned without Dutch aid, and a piecemeal system of licensing grew up, especially towards the end of the Protectorate. The rest of the colonies were largely left alone, including Guiana and Surinam, acquired in 1650. The colonial tobacco industry received definite support from the state. An Act passed in 1652 prohibited tobacco planting in England (there were sizeable plantations in Gloucestershire and Worcestershire), and efforts were made to enforce it. Privateering and sugar-growing were actively encouraged, and indeed the experts upon whom the Protectorate Government most relied for advice upon the economic affairs of the nation were West India merchants. Several committees were established to deal with aspects of the colonial trade and a Board of Trade and Navigation was said by Whitelocke to have been "a business of much concern to the Commonwealth, upon which the Protector was earnestly set".

Apart from that, the governments of the colonies were virtually left alone. A known Royalist was allowed to continue as governor of Surinam throughout the Protectorate, and the colonists had little difficulty in evading commercial and fiscal regulations which they disliked. Cromwell tried to arbitrate in boundary disputes between Maryland and Virginia and between Rhode Island and other colonies, and on the whole his methods were conciliatory. In 1654 he sent a small expedition to New England to try to help capture Dutch settlements from a base in Massachusetts, but nothing came of this, as the force arrived from England just as peace was concluded. However, the expedition sailed on to the coast of Acadia and occupied territory in French hands, now known as Nova Scotia, a province of Canada. Cromwell approved of the acquisition which had been lost in the reign of Charles I, and also put forward other claims to Canadian territory during the Anglo-French negotiations of 1654 and 1655. Settlements in India and Africa were left in the hands of joint stock companies for the purpose of increasing trade.

It would be wrong and anachronistic to say that Cromwell and his advisers had any clear "colonial policy" as such. The fact was, to use a modern word that is often abused, he and his officials were imperialists. Theirs was an age of restless expansion. All the colonies in America and the West Indies had been established in Cromwell's own lifetime. But whether he was proposing to obtain Dunkirk or Calais or Bremen by war, whether he was urging Blake to take Gibraltar from the Spaniards or Admiral Penn to occupy San Domingo or make for Cuba, whether he was settling his former soldiers in colonies in Ireland, as the Romans had once done in England, or dispatching prisoners to populate the West Indies or become indentured servants in Massachusetts, it was all part of the same impulse to expand England's power and influence throughout the world, to propagate the true reformed religion, to widen the markets for English goods and to build up a source of supplies for the home market, and to insure against the return of the Stuarts. He was no Little Englander or universal Free Trader. He was not, though we may be inclined to forget it, an Eminent Victorian, nor did he live in our own contracting globe. The Navigation Acts were aimed at the increase of British shipping and the strengthening of the British Navy. The great trading companies, like the West India Company and the Levant Company, were also regarded as national instruments, being expected to provide ambassadors, to build forts, and to hire soldiers to protect and widen English trade in Asia and other distant parts. In a famous phrase he told his last parliament : "You have accounted yourselves happy in being environed with a great ditch from all the world beside. Truly you will not be able to keep your ditch, nor your shipping—unless you turn your ships and shipping into troops of horse and companies of foot; and fight to defend yourselves in *terra firma*!"

This robust outlook guided his conduct in the last years of his Protectorate. The war with Spain was relentlessly pursued at sea. In September 1656, a Spanish treasure fleet was destroyed or captured off Cadiz. (It is said that the Cromwellian coins made from some of the captured silver and designed by Thomas Simon are among the most beautiful known to British collectors.) In April 1657, Blake won a big victory off Santa Cruz, causing a loss which meant that the Spanish soldiers were starved of their pay, and about the same time an offensive treaty was signed with France, whereby the English government undertook to provide an expeditionary force to fight alongside the French against the Spaniards in Flanders, and to receive the ports of Mardyke and Dunkirk in return as soon as they were captured.

Cromwell's "redcoats" served with distinction in the campaigns of 1657 and 1658. Marshal Turenne, the famous French general, commended their gallant conduct at the battle of the Dunes in June 1658. The French monarchy was naturally not anxious to fulfil its promises made in the treaty, for it did not relish the idea of having a British Republican fortress so near to its frontier. But Cromwell insisted that Mardyke and Dunkirk must be handed over, condemning French excuses as "parcels of words for children", and so, before he died, he had won his door into the Continent.

Cromwell also contemplated sending an expeditionary force to the help of King Charles X of Sweden. He demanded Bremen in return for his services in the same way that he had obtained Dunkirk from King Louis XIV. When in 1657, Charles X was confronted by a coalition which included the Habsburg emperor, Cromwell was conscious of the danger that the Habsburgs might overwhelm the Protestants of northern Europe and reverse the results of the Thirty Years War. In fact, the Protestants were divided amongst themselves, since the Danes and Brandenburgers were also engaged against Sweden, while in the south the French Catholics were fighting beside the English Puritans against the Spanish Habsburgs. The days of religious wars were ending. Cromwell himself was aware that a victorious Sweden might again exclude British shipping from the Baltic, and that it was safer that the sound should remain under Danish control. However, he made promises of paying Charles X a subsidy; he allowed him to recruit soldiers in Scotland, and, to give him countenance, he prepared to dispatch an English fleet to the Baltic; above all, he exerted diplomatic pressure to induce the Swedes and Danes to conclude peace, as they did temporarily in February 1658, after English mediation. In any case, the Protectorate Government had not the resources to fight in northern and southern Europe simultaneously, while the northern war was a death-blow to the ambitious scheme for a Protestant alliance against the Habsburgs.

Thus, when Oliver Cromwell died, England was an acknowledged Great Power in the world, with her prestige higher upon the Continent of Europe even than in Queen Elizabeth's golden days. John Dryden wrote in his poem upon Cromwell's death:

> *"He made us free men of the Continent*
> *Whom nations did like captives treat before;*
> *To nobler prizes the English lion sent*
> *And taught him first in Belgian walks to roar."*

"Cromwell's greatness at home," admitted his Royalist enemy, the first Earl of Clarendon, "was but a shadow of the glory he had abroad." He had given his country a position of impressive strength, broad-based upon an experienced army and a magnificent navy, which had made the British name respected in the Mediterranean. Cromwell himself appreciated the importance of sea-power, as most great British generals have done. Edmund Waller could write:

> *"Others may use the ocean as their road,*
> *Only the English make it their abode."*

The military occupation of Dunkirk, which "once more joined us to the Continent", bridled both the Dutch and the Spaniards, while the French, who had let it fall into British hands, had most reason to regret it. Farther abroad, the foundations had been laid for British expansion in the West Indies, in Canada, and in what was to become in the next century the United States of America. Daring projects filled Oliver Cromwell's mind—for the annexation of Cuba, for example, or a settlement in Brazil. The Protestant interest, the central theme of his speeches on foreign policy, was allied to a patriotism that he took for granted, and to an unblushing imperialism sanctified by Christianity. We may suspect that the abuse of Republicans at home and of the Royalists abroad meant little to this inspired statesman, as compared with the exhilarating dreams he dreamed of the future magnificence of his country. He was dreaming them still as his life reached its close.

Chapter Thirteen

The Fall of the Republic

WHILE in the year 1658 the prestige of the English Commonwealth under the Protectorate of Oliver Cromwell never stood so high in Europe, the situation at home was confused. Rumours persisted that King Charles II was planning an invasion with a cavalry force of eight thousand men, and that the younger Royalists were plotting a rising in the City of London and the south of England. The City militia was called up, a number of conspirators were arrested and two of them put to death, and the reports received from England by the exiled Court discouraged any idea of invasion. By the spring all was more or less quiet, and the Privy Council was busily discussing whether a new parliament should be summoned in the autumn and another effort made to induce Cromwell to become King. But the Privy Council was as divided over home affairs as it had been over foreign policy. A few members, headed by John Desborough, wanted a return to the rule of major-generals; a majority favoured calling a new parliament, but was uncertain whether to recommend reviving monarchy in Cromwell's family. It is likely that Cromwell himself, still searching for a constitutional settlement, inclined that way; at any rate, the well-informed French ambassador reported in March that "the re-establishment of royalty is determined on". Moreover, the Lord Protector received no agreed advice. In the previous summer, Henry Cromwell's father-in-law had written to him that the Council was so unhelpful that the Lord Protector was obliged to rely upon his own judgment. "He counsels himself were it not so, lo, I know not what would become of things." The correspondence between Henry Cromwell, who had now been appointed Lord Lieutenant of Ireland, and John Thurloe, Cromwell's sole Secretary of State, opens a window upon the hopes and fears of Cromwell's immediate entourage. Their opinion was that a policy of conciliation was the best, that a parliament should be called, and full use made of the victories won abroad to fortify the Lord Protector's position. At the same time they agreed that for peace at home they must rely entirely upon his personal influence. For he was widely trusted even by men who differed from him over policy. "Does not your peace," asked Henry Cromwell in June, "depend upon his Highness's life, and upon his peculiar skill and faculty and personal interest in the army as now modelled and commanded?" Thurloe thought that Cromwell himself would have to make up his own mind "and not so much consider others".

Thus, after nearly six years of experimenting in different forms of government, it was still purely upon his own personal leadership that Cromwell's friends and advisers depended for peace and the survival of the Commonwealth. Leadership is hard to define, but its reality was clear to Cromwell's contemporaries. Andrew Marvell wrote of Cromwell that he seemed "a king by long succession born", but went on to say :

> *"Abroad a king he seems and something more,*
> *At home a subject on an equal floor."*

Foreigners recognized his greatness more plainly than Englishmen : a woman of perception like Queen Christina of Sweden could see it, as could a vigilant statesman like Mazarin. At home Cromwell's republican enemies, such as Haselrigg and Edmund Ludlow, thought of him as just another amateur soldier like themselves whose success as a statesman they ascribed to hypocrisy and devouring personal ambition. But to those who actually served under him—George Monk, John Thurloe, John Milton—his power and influence required no such explanation. He was their "chief of men". Cromwell's Royalist opponent, the Earl of Clarendon, besides paying tribute to his reputation abroad, spoke of "his great spirit, admirable sagacity, and most magnanimous resolution". He also declared that he was not "a man of blood" nor a disciple of Machiavelli. Another Royalist observed that "had his cause been good", Cromwell would have counted as "one of the greatest and bravest men the world ever produced".

Such contemporaries (and the eighteenth-century biographers who took their evidence mostly from his critics) judged him chiefly in secular terms. For example, a Venetian envoy wrote of him in 1656 that "it cannot be denied that by his ability and industry he has contributed to his own greatness". He spoke, too, of his courage, good sense, and prudence. The same sort of compliments might have been paid to other men of the time—to Lambert, to Thurloe, or to Monk. Where Cromwell differed from them was in his blinding sense of vocation, in the belief to which he gradually and reluctantly came that he alone could save his country from anarchy or invasion. He drew his strength from his religion, counting always upon the infinite love of God, and upon that covenant made with men whereby the Almighty "undertakes all and the poor soul nothing". Even this sense of inner fortitude, like Cromwell's "industry, courage, and prudence", would have meant nothing if he had not also possessed the gift of commanding loyalty.

Cromwell's methods were never those of a tyrant. He wrestled with other men's consciences as well as his own; he tried to understand their difficulties, spiritual, moral or even political; he never thought that he had a monopoly of the truth. In the last years of his life he acquired an extraordinary degree of tolerance, unique in his time: "From his agonies and his exaltations," it has been said, "he emerged with a great charity towards men." A word that was frequently used about him, not only by his friends but by his critics, was "magnanimity". It was because of that great-heartedness of his that, even if they did not understand his mysticism and were puzzled by his inconsistencies as a statesman, most of his soldiers and administrators always trusted him. Thus he kept his power virtually intact until the end of his days. Not that he ever obtained much happiness from it; only the call of duty beckoned him on; he never expected peace until after he was dead.

By the early spring of 1658 his health was beginning to fail, as was shown by a signature already crabbed with premature old age. He had never recovered from the illnesses contracted during the Irish and Scottish campaigns, and his sense of direct responsibility weighed upon him. "The difficulties of his place," wrote one of his servants, "was so great a burden . . . as I doubt not to say it drank up his spirits (of which his natural constitution yielded a vast stock) and brought him to his grave." He died on the afternoon of 3 September, after nominating his son Richard as his successor.

To understand the articulation of political affairs in the last months of Oliver Cromwell's life, it must be realized that a number of parties existed in the Commonwealth, though they shaded imperceptibly into one another. In the first place was the army. Ever since 1647 this had, in effect, been a third estate of the realm. Chiefly Independent in its religious opinions, it had formed a counterpoise to parliament which, in whatever form it had met (except for the Assembly of Saints), contained a substantial number of men sympathetic to the Presbyterian point of view. The army on the whole was republican, but believed in a strong executive. Secondly, there were the oligarchic republicans led by Haselrigg, Vane, and Thomas Scot, with some friends in the army such as Colonel Edmund Ludlow. A small group of democratic republicans also existed, though they had been weakened by the death of John Lilburne, the Leveller leader, in 1657; his successor, John Wildman, had combined intriguing with the Royalists and spying for the government. Next came the group of New Cromwellians, who were still urging Oliver to accept the Crown. They, however, lacked organized leadership. Lord Broghill, their most notable member, and Lord Falconbridge, one of Cromwell's sons-in-law, were suspect because they had formerly been Royalists; while John Thurloe, though a highly capable administrator, lacked courage and finesse as a politician. But all these groups respected the Lord

Protector. The situation was bound to deteriorate after his death.

At first Richard Cromwell was upheld by his father's ghost. "No civil war broils have since his death arose," wrote Dryden optimistically, "but Fashion now by habit does obey." "There is not a dog that wags his tongue," observed Thurloe, "so great a calm are we in." Speaking of Charles II, Sir Edward Hyde said : "The King's condition never appeared so hopeless, so desperate." But it was not long before Richard Cromwell was in trouble. His chief difficulty was that, never having been a soldier, except for a short time, he commanded little influence in the army. His brother-in-law, General Charles Fleetwood, was jealous of him, and the suggestion was soon put forward that Fleetwood ought to be appointed commander-in-chief, while Richard retained only the title of Lord Protector; but Richard Cromwell, who was by no means unpopular with those who knew him, understood clearly enough that if he let go his control over the army he would become its prisoner.

The new Lord Protector decided not to make any important changes in the composition of the Privy Council that he had inherited from his father; neither Broghill nor Falconbridge, leaders of the New Cromwellians, were admitted to it; only Edward Montagu, who was now in effect in command of the Commonwealth navy, was a Councillor with influence in the armed forces, ready to uphold the Protectorate at all costs. Richard's two wisest advisers and most loyal supporters, his brother Henry and George Monk, commanded for him in Ireland and Scotland respectively, and could only send him advice by letter. If he had brought them both to London, he might well have saved his throne. As it was, Monk offered astute suggestions. He told him that he ought to reduce the size of the army and, by amalgamating regiments, get rid of senior officers whose loyalty was in doubt. Similarly, he should make changes in the naval commands and, in general, remodel the armed forces so that he could be assured of their unswerving support. Monk also thought that he would do well to strengthen the discipline of the

Church and call moderate Presbyterians into his counsels. He warned him to think carefully before calling parliament, to try to persuade some of the hereditary peerage to enter his House of Lords, and to rely upon the New Cromwellians, including Broghill and Thurloe, as his principal advisers. The main objection to such recommendations as these was that for Richard Cromwell to turn now to the Presbyterians would have been to compromise with his father's policy of toleration, while only Monk himself was capable of remodelling the armed forces, since Fleetwood, Desborough, and the rest were already beginning to intrigue against the new Protector. It is not known what Richard thought of Monk's advice. In any case, he did not follow it. The policy that he did adopt, apparently under the guidance of Thurloe, was quite different and was fatal to him.

During October and November the army showed itself exceptionally restless. Fleetwood had the effrontery to present the new Lord Protector with a petition, inviting him to give up his office of commander-in-chief, and the demand was also put forward that the officers whom Oliver Cromwell had cashiered for disloyalty should be restored to their commands. Richard pointed out that he had already nominated Fleetwood as lieutenant-general to command immediately under him, while he promised that no officers should be promoted without the advice of his Privy Council and none should be arbitrarily dismissed. This conciliatory policy failed to satisfy the army malcontents, many of whom were justifiably aggrieved because their pay was in arrears. The decision taken to call parliament in January 1659 was undoubtedly influenced by the consideration that it might prove a counter-balance to the army and might vote supplies that would enable the new Protector to meet his and his father's debts.

Richard Cromwell's parliament was summoned under the constitution known as the "Petition and Advice", which had been agreed to in 1657. Thus the constituency reforms introduced by the "Instrument of Government" were abandoned and the property qualification for voting in the counties reduced. This somewhat altered the character of the House of Commons, which, when it met, did not prove unfriendly to the Protector himself but was vehemently anti-military in its attitude. It is possible that as many as two-thirds of the members were willing to vote for the government at a pinch, but, as in the two previous parliaments, Sir Arthur Haselrigg had a following of over fifty out-and-out republicans, a small group craved for true democracy, and John Lambert, who had quarrelled with Oliver Cromwell in 1657, represented the army republicans. A few concealed Royalists also managed to find their way into the House, with the aim of creating mischief. The late Dr. Godfrey Davies summed up the situation in these words : "A Protectorate limited by the Humble Petition and Advice was preferred to a republic, a republic to the sword."

Once again, as in the previous Protectorate parliaments, all the skill and oratory in the House was to be found in the avowed republican opposition. The Court party was outmanœuvred and out-debated. Haselrigg at once threw down his challenge by telling the new Speaker that he "looked upon him as the greatest man in England". Thurloe committed a grave error of judgment by introducing a Bill for the recognition of the new Protector. For this gave Haselrigg the precise opportunity that he had exploited so cleverly during earlier parliaments, to set the House by its ears. Once more constitution-mongering was used as an excellent excuse to ignore every other need of the country, to vote no taxes, and to promote no reforms. The past was acrimoniously gone over again in every detail : the origins of the civil wars, the misdeeds of Oliver Cromwell, the cowardice of the House of Lords, the grievances of individual members, the betrayal of the "good old cause" of the republic were all aired. Moreover, exactly the same tactics were adopted to embarrass the government as had been tried unsuccessfully against Oliver. A petition was organized in the City of London and presented to the House, designed to please both the straightlaced republicans, the old Leveller sympathizers, and the rank-and-file of the army. It had been a similar petition that provoked Oliver to dissolve the last parliament. Richard took it on the chin, and for the time being the storm passed over.

The opposition now concentrated upon constitutional matters, interspersed with violent attacks upon the army. Military rule was denounced, the conduct and even the loyalty of the soldiers were called into question, and one of the former major-generals of the horse militia was impeached. Although the Protector was recognized, no serious attempt was made to meet his wishes, either for assistance in paying for the continuing war against Spain or to appease the army by meeting its arrears. After three months the members themselves began to grow bored with the arid constitutional discussions, but the baiting of the army did not diminish and the consequence was to be expected.

So restless had the army become by the beginning of April 1659 that Fleetwood asked permission of Richard Cromwell to call a General Council. Five hundred officers met on 2 April. Richard Cromwell's friends tried to persuade the meeting that the best plan would be to trust the Protector to put matters right. The majority, however, decided to draw up a petition outlining their complaints. This petition pointed out that want of pay might compel soldiers to live at "free quarter", that law suits had been started against officers merely for obeying orders, and that the Cavaliers were being encouraged. The army demanded its arrears and asked that freedom of worship, threatened by the Presbyterians in the Commons, should be re-affirmed. Richard Cromwell forwarded this petition to both Houses : the House of Commons ignored it for some days, and then resolved that while it would try to settle the financial problem, no further Councils of the army should on any account be allowed to meet.

So matters had reached the point where the Lord Protector had to decide whether he would side with parliament against the army, or the army against parliament— his father's earliest dilemma. Since Richard knew that he commanded little influence with the leaders of the army, while he still had a measure of support in the Commons, he plucked up his courage and told Fleetwood and Desborough that the army must stop its meetings as the Commons required, and when he received a refusal he ordered their arrest. But no one would obey his orders, not even his own bodyguard. The same evening Desborough went to see Richard Cromwell in Whitehall, and told him brutally that he must dissolve parliament or take the consequences. After vainly asking permission to consult members of his Privy Council, Richard crumpled under threats, and that was, in fact, the end of the Protectorate. Since Fleetwood and Desborough were both connected to him by marriage, it was said that his own family had destroyed him.

It was not really as simple as that. The Protectorate had been overthrown by the same combination of enemies that had vainly conspired against Oliver Cromwell. While the filibustering of Haselrigg had angered the army, the republicans inside the House of Commons had acted in concert with a powerful republican section in the army, linked by Colonel Ludlow, who was an M.P. and had always been the implacable opponent of the Protectorate. Though the army was their instrument and perhaps their dupe, it was the irreconcilable republicans who broke the Cromwellian Protectorate. That fact was underlined by what happened afterwards. Fleetwood and his friends had intended to keep the Protectorate in being, to use Richard Cromwell as their tool, and themselves to govern without parliament. But since Richard Cromwell, by his feebleness and final reluctance to rule, had become a wasting asset, since the army itself was split between its official leadership and the republican rank-and-file (much as it had been in 1647), and since Fleetwood and his friends had thought of no new system of government to replace the Protectorate, they now found themselves obliged to come to an agreement with the parliamentary republicans. At a meeting on 2 May it was settled that the Rump Parliament should be recalled and the oligarchic government of the early sixteen-fifties restored. The Rump met on 7 May, and on 25 May Richard Cromwell submitted to it and retired into private life.

The complicated and unedifying story of the fall of

Richard Cromwell has been told at some length (even though its details today are not entirely plain), because it throws a flood of light backwards upon the historical place of Oliver Cromwell. The Rump of some fifty or sixty politicians who now insisted upon their indefeasible right to rule the country in uneasy alliance with the army, several of whom had first been elected to the Commons nearly twenty years earlier, were, as Sir Charles Firth wrote, "the Bourbons of republicanism". Twenty-one of its members were appointed to the new Council of State, and thus the administration was put into the hands of a narrow oligarchy, lacking in genuine leadership, experience, or public credit, and behaving "like tired, irritable men". It was impossible, after what had gone before, that men like Haselrigg and Vane could command any loyalty in the army, which they tried to purge and remodel. Even Monk, who wrote from Scotland professing obedience to the new civil power, vainly asked that changes in his army there should not be made without his own consent. Such was the confusion and distrust manifested among the former conquerors of King Charles I that a new Royalist rising and a new *coup d'état* by the army obviously had become only questions of time. Oliver had kept the army under control by a combination of personal magnetism and discipline, while seeking a constitutional settlement that allowed for a balanced form of government prescribed by written laws and eschewing arbitrary devices. It is true that the judges and lawyers had never liked the "Instrument of Government" because they refused to recognize its legal basis, but, as compared with the system of Puritan government envisaged by the "Instrument" and later by the "Humble Petition and Advice", the shaky oligarchy of the returned Rump combined every political disadvantage : it was unpopular, it was muddled, and it was ineffective. If it is the fact, as has so often been asserted, that Oliver Cromwell could not govern with parliaments nor without them, the republican oligarchs could neither govern with the army nor without it. "Chaos," it was said not unfairly by a contemporary Royalist, "was a perfection compared to our present order and government." As soon as the Royalists rose again, as they did in August 1659, the utter dependence of the parliament on the army, for all its brave words, became crystal clear.

Colonel John Lambert was the man who, after defeating this Royalist rising, essayed to become another Oliver Cromwell. Though he was a good soldier, an able political thinker, and a proved administrator, he lacked many of the gifts of his great predecessor. He was not in any obvious sense of the term a Puritan, and his personal ambitions made him the target of suspicion. Not being given the rewards he expected after his victory over the Royalists, he returned to his home in Yorkshire, where he indulged in a fit of sulking, ignoring orders to come to London. Soon after he eventually arrived there, a petition was sent up to the Rump Parliament from the officers of his army stationed in Derby, asking that Fleetwood should be appointed commander-in-chief, with full powers, and that Lambert himself should be restored to his previous post of major-general, which had already been denied him. Fleetwood was ordered to suppress this petition (which General Monk in Scotland had refused to allow the men in his army to support), and on 5 October a new petition was put forward by another group of army officers, which included the requirement that no officer might be cashiered except by court martial or by order of the local commander. Parliament retorted by cashiering Lambert and eight other high-ranking officers, and vesting the control of the army in a number of commissioners.

After the defeat of their rising, the Royalists had become depressed. The policy was now tried of suborning Commonwealth commanders from their loyalties. The suggestion was put forward that Lambert's daughter, Mary, a pretty girl "of extraordinary sweetness of disposition", should marry Charles II's brother, the Duke of York, and General Monk's brother, an Anglican clergyman, was sent up to Edinburgh to offer him £100,000 if he would transfer his services to the exiled King. Monk, like Lambert, was no Puritan—"he had no fancies of religion which turned his head", so Sir Edward Hyde wrote—but he had a reputation for being fond of money. Fleetwood, though Puritan enough, was known to be a weakling, usually siding with the last person to whom he spoke, and was not taken into much account. Thus the future seemed to rest between two non-Puritan generals who each had a considerable following in the army.

The first move was made by Lambert who, on 13 October, led a contingent to Westminster and dissolved the Rump by force, setting up a Committee of Safety to replace the Council of State. But Monk, as soon as he heard this news, decided to march to London in defence of the Rump. He "told Lambert in so many words that what he was prepared to tolerate in Oliver Cromwell he could not stomach in a lesser man". Monk purged his own army of all officers he suspected of not being personally loyal to himself, and concentrated his force upon the Scottish frontier. Meanwhile a Republican rising took place in London, Fleetwood threw up the sponge, and Haselrigg returned in triumph with the garrison of Portsmouth. On the day after Christmas, the Rump met again in Westminster, while Lambert's army, unpaid and without supplies, melted away from him, and Monk advanced unopposed through York, where he was welcomed with enthusiasm by the retired commander-in-chief, Lord Fairfax. As Monk moved slowly across England, addresses were received by him from all over the country, demanding the calling of "a free parliament", and hearty demonstrations took place in favour of King Charles II. The City of London, which had greeted the two restorations of the Rump with equal apathy and had refused to grant financial aid to the government, now announced that it would pay no further taxes until the attenuated House of Commons filled its vacancies. Monk, when he arrived in the capital, was ordered to enforce obedience upon the City; he did so, but then "was dark, and chewed his tobacco", and eventually, impressed by the wave of feeling in London and elsewhere in favour of the Stuarts, took the decision, like Cromwell, Desborough, and Lambert before him, to turn his sword against the civil power. He told the Rump to admit its secluded members and not to sit beyond

6 May 1660, so that "a free parliament" might be elected. Meanwhile, he entered into direct communication with King Charles II. When, under his supervision, the new parliament or Convention met, it invited the King to come home again.

So, in the end, the restoration of the Stuart line came without bloodshed. As we read the dismal story of the last days of the English Commonwealth, we are conscious that the Puritan impulse that gave it its original moral strength had departed; no one showed any concern about liberty of conscience, and no one played a part that was in the least heroic. Nothing remained but a small group of ambitious generals and jealous oligarchs, struggling with one another for power. A few intellectual republicans, like Vane and James Harrington, were engaged in working out wonderful paper constitutions while their world fell in upon them. In retrospect, the revolution appeared to have come to its real end when Oliver Cromwell died. Those of his contemporaries and later historians who claimed that he himself had betrayed the revolution when he dismissed the Rump in December 1653, ought to have reflected upon what actually happened when the Rump resumed power in 1659, and how totally incapable it showed itself to be either of controlling the army or governing the country, even when it had a loyal general at its disposal.

But one significant event happened before King Charles II returned to England. In May 1660, when the Convention had assembled, letters were read to it from the King, together with a declaration signed by him at Breda. In this declaration the King promised that he would leave to a future parliament many major decisions of policy, and also proclaimed "we do declare a liberty to tender consciences". Those who heard those words, while hoping for the settled government that Oliver Cromwell had never completely achieved, might surely have believed that the revolution had not been entirely in vain.

Chapter Fourteen

What the Puritan Revolution Achieved

WHAT did the Puritan Revolution achieve? Did it in fact achieve anything at all? In our standard history books the question is surprisingly little discussed. The year 1660 is taken almost as a closed frontier in historical time or a safety-curtain lowered after a play that is best forgotten. It was a revolution that failed, had it not? For King Charles II was restored unconditionally and by the very army that had once followed Oliver Cromwell. Nothing of importance, we are instructed, was retained out of all the legislation and political activity of the years between 1642, when King Charles I left his capital, and May 1660, when his son returned there. Most of the conclusions that are offered us come in negatives : Cromwell "had not succeeded in making Puritanism admirable to the majority of Englishmen" or "England had repudiated the Puritan attempt to enforce strict morality by the use of the army".

It would hardly be credible that this revolution, in which so much blood and fire and passion were expended, should have left no mark whatever upon British history. It would be astonishing if all the political experiments, all the philosophical thinking, all the religious exuberance, all the written constitutions and different governments of those eighteen years had made no impression whatsoever upon the minds of men; or if the character of Oliver Cromwell, which, even upon the tercentenary of his death, divides the judgments of historians and arouses journalists to display contradictory opinions, contributed nothing to the moulding of later society.

To take the obvious points first. It is not entirely true that the legislation of the Interregnum left no traces in the statute book. To give two examples : important reforms of the law (which Cromwell had so much at heart) were retained; it was confirmed that in the future the language of the Common Law courts should be English and not French or dog Latin, and also that a defendant might enter a general plea of "not guilty", and so be able to join issue at once without preliminary production of evidence in bar of an action. Secondly, the series of Navigation Acts introduced after the Restoration were merely an extension of the navigation laws carried through and enforced during the Interregnum. They had the same objects : to enable shipowners and shippers to compete more effectively with their chief commercial rivals, the Dutch, in the carrying trade, and to promote Britain's business intercourse with her colonies. Maybe none of these Acts were soundly designed for their purpose (though in the twentieth century we are less dogmatic about Protection than our grandfathers), but at least they exemplify a striking continuation of policy.

Among other concrete survivals from the Interregnum are two of our most famous historical regiments, the Coldstream Guards—direct descendants of the Ironsides—and the Grenadier Guards. The greatness of the British Navy may also be said to date largely from the Cromwellian era; for, if it was founded by King Henry VIII and built up by Queen Elizabeth I, it won some of its most notable victories in the Dutch and Spanish wars. Nearly half the Lord Protector's revenue was spent upon the navy; it was the foundation which allowed Britain to become a great power in the seventeenth century, and from the time of Robert Blake it kept a continuous station in the Mediterranean. Blake and Monk in their different ways were commanders of great ability. After the Restoration, Monk, Penn, Batten, and other naval officers continued to serve the monarchy and uphold the Commonwealth traditions. The new tactics, principally invented by Blake and Monk, were pursued when war came, and it was naval prestige, won during the Protectorate, that encouraged King

Charles II's government to try conclusions with the Dutch, though less successfully than before.

It was not only at sea that the services of Commonwealth administrators were employed. Indeed, it was under Cromwell that capable men with something approaching a Civil Service cast of mind were employed by the executive, instead of rich men who bought their offices and left most of the duties to their underlings. The alliance with France was affirmed, the wars with the Dutch resumed, the connection with Portugal was strengthened. Some of the colonial conquests from Spain were maintained. Jamaica, it has been said, became the "pet colony" of the Restoration. Thence were exported coffee, sugar, and pepper, and the island became an excellent market for English manufactured goods. Buccaneering, as was anticipated during the Interregnum, became a profitable industry, and from Jamaica the headquarters of Spanish trade in Central America was sacked. But not all the conquests of the Cromwellian era were retained; the union with Scotland (provided for in "The Instrument of Government") was abandoned; in October 1662 Dunkirk was sold to France, a step that was very unpopular at the time and helped to bring about the downfall of King Charles II's minister, the first Earl of Clarendon, who was believed to have advised the sale. Acadia was surrendered to the Dutch in 1667, although later it was regained. The gradual decline in English prestige abroad during the reigns of King Charles II and King James II, a fact to which attention was first drawn in a famous pamphlet by Andrew Marvell, who had served under Thurloe during the Protectorate, was extremely damaging to the Stuarts; even the most loyal Royalists looked back sadly to the "great days of Oliver". It was not until the Dutchman, King William III, ascended the throne in 1689 that the rulers of England and France again became equals.

Although the restoration of King Charles II was unconditional, the intention of parliament was to return to the constitutional position of 1642 and not of 1640. Though no mention was made of legislation passed during the first year of the Long Parliament, it was tacitly and implicitly confirmed; for only the later ordinances of the Long Parliament, which had not received the assent of King Charles I, were specifically declared invalid. Thus the Tudor Royal courts, the dubious methods of raising taxes, the imprisonments without cause shown, and other exercises in the use of prerogative power were all swept away. Moreover, though the Triennial Act, which Oliver Cromwell had helped to introduce, was repealed, a new one required the King to summon a fresh parliament three years after a previous one had been dissolved. King Charles II could, therefore, only tax his subjects with parliament's consent; justice was confined to the Common Law courts and the Court of Chancery; and in effect the jurisdiction of the ecclesiastical courts was much more limited than it had been before the civil wars.

The privileges of the House of Commons were now finally recognized by the Crown. A historian has recently written that at the Restoration, "the old unity of 'King in Parliament' was replaced by a new trinity of 'Kings, Lords, and Commons', and the replacement was perhaps only unchallenged because it was clothed in a restoration". The growing independence of the House of Commons was accepted. The Long Parliament or Pensionary Parliament of King Charles II's reign which, when it met, was enthusiastically Royalist, became, after the initial failures of the government in foreign and domestic policy, hostile in temper ten years later, even though its original membership had not been substantially changed. Constitutional advance is, after all, always dictated by political facts. The structure of parliament was probably not materially altered. King Charles II may have tried to pick his later parliaments, but he did not dare to defy them indefinitely as his father had done. King James II found he was unable to pick or pack a parliament which he needed to promote his own religious ends. Both men were forewarned by the fate of their father. The bloody revolution of 1649 was the prelude to the bloodless revolution of forty years later, when King James II preferred to escape in a yacht to France rather than to fight another civil war. If it is true, as Mr. David Ogg has written, that in some respects

Charles II was a constitutional monarch, that was because he never forgot that parliament had beaten his father and he did not intend to go into exile again.

Charles II was an agreeable, accessible, highly intelligent man. No one can say with confidence, any more than one can say of any man, that he was completely devoid of moral principles, but the behaviour of his Court set lax standards. When he married his Portuguese Queen, he at once insisted that his principal mistress should be made her Lady of the Bedchamber. He promoted men not because of their inherent capacities, but, as in the case of the second Duke of Buckingham, because they were amusing companions. He winked at piracies and robberies if the pirates or robbers happened to entertain him. Like the rest of the Stuarts, he had little sense of personal loyalty; he was indolent and extravagant, and his gay Court was a centre of vice. It has often been pointed out that there were many respectable and devoted men and women among the servants of King Charles II, but the Court set the tone to society, and corruption flourished in the administration in a way that it never did when Oliver Cromwell lived in Whitehall.

If the pattern of society changed during the reign of King Charles II, the Church was even more violently affected by the Restoration. The many Presbyterians who had assisted in bringing back the King had assumed that a place would be found for them in the ecclesiastical settlement. In the autumn of 1656 a scheme for combining Presbyterian and episcopal government, invented by Archbishop Ussher of Armagh, had been published, and many Presbyterians hoped that as the price for their aid they would be comprehended within the Church of England. In fact, it was the Laudians, headed by Dr. Gilbert Sheldon, Bishop of London, who, having carefully prepared the way during the Interregnum, triumphed after Charles II's return. William Laud, the High Church Archbishop of Canterbury, who had been beheaded on Tower Hill in 1645, like Samson, slew more Puritans by his death than he ever did in his life. The resurgent Laudianism of the Restoration was, however, devoid of any social or political content; it was a purely ecclesiastical victory. At the Savoy conference, held in the Bishop of London's lodgings in 1660, the Presbyterian leaders, badly led, were outmanœuvred, and by the Act of Uniformity of 1661, a revised Book of Common Prayer was imposed upon all clergy, who were compelled to sign a declaration promising to adopt the new book and to repudiate the Solemn League and Covenant. Thus the Presbyterians, together with the dissenters or sectarians, were driven out of the Church. It has been estimated that 2,000 out of 10,000 parochial clergy resigned their livings, and when, on St. Bartholomew's Day, 1662, they gave up their benefices, nonconformity took permanent shape.

The Act of Uniformity was buttressed by a number of other measures known collectively as "the Clarendon Code". By the Conventicle Act, if five or more persons met for religious purposes the meeting was declared illegal, and transportation was the penalty for the third offence. By the Five Mile Act, all men in holy orders who did not take the prescribed oaths were forbidden to teach or preach in corporate towns. Another Act allowed constables to break into houses where it was suspected that nonconformists met. The reason for this panic legislation was because the government feared that the nonconformists were plotting another revolution under the cover of religion. This was far from being the case. But a heavy blow had been delivered against the Presbyterians; some of them joined the Church of England, took the oaths, and created a kind of Low Church movement. Others allied with their old enemies, the Independents or Congregationalists. And, in reaction against the violence of both sides in the former religious conflict, a Broad or Latitudinarian movement began in the Church, with which a former brother-in-law of Oliver Cromwell, Dr. Wilkins, Bishop of Chester, was associated.

Though dissent continued to flourish in those areas where the magistrates were sympathetic and therefore did not strictly enforce the Clarendon Code, undoubtedly the Code was damaging to the nonconformists. According to one estimate, there were in the reign of King Charles II only about 150,000 of them left out of a total population of over five millions. When one considers how Puritanism had coloured the whole life of the country in the Cromwellian era, this is a strikingly low figure, if it can be believed. But whatever they lacked in numbers, the nonconformists made up in tenacity and variety; when the Grand Duke of Tuscany visited the country he was astounded at the diversity of religious beliefs. Naturally, one must not underestimate the strain to which they were subjected by the persecution under the Clarendon Code. A recent writer on Puritanism in that period has hazarded the opinion that it injured them permanently, and that, after the smoke of battle cleared in 1689, their "old resiliency of spirit" had disappeared. But if the religious side of nonconformity suffered, its political, economic and, above all, social influence remained strong, if indirect. Though the nonconformists could take no part in public life, they formed a pressure group as early as the eighteenth century. Above all, the Puritan Revolution brought to birth the nonconformist conscience, which ripened during the struggles under the later Stuarts, came to maturity in the reign of Queen Anne, and permeated middle-class society, regardless of creed, in the reign of Queen Victoria.

The severity of the Clarendon Code was explained by the fear of the government that the dissenters might take advantage of the confusion caused by the second Dutch war (1664-7), the Great Plague (1665), and the Great Fire of London (1666), to plot a fresh revolution; but they were never sufficiently powerful or united to contemplate any such action. True, they were disappointed, especially after the promises of indulgence given by the King himself in the early years of his reign, that they were not allowed to attend their chapels peacefully under their own ministers, while the Presbyterians believed that they had been betrayed. But in so far as republican plotting continued after the Restoration, it was in the spirit of Haselrigg, Ludlow, and the keener secular politicians, and was not specifically religious in its inspiration.

King Charles II declared himself to be a Roman Catholic upon his death-bed in 1685, and his brother had long

been an open adherent of that religion when he came to
the throne as King James II. It was a remarkable historical *volte-face*. That less than thirty years after Oliver
Cromwell was buried and much more than a century
after Queen Mary I died, a new Roman Catholic ruler
should succeed peacefully to the thrones of both England
and Scotland postulated a degree of religious apathy and
a weakening in the national character that contrasted
strangely with all the passion and excitement of the Interregnum.

Yet a flash of the old spirit soon disclosed that whatever
promises the new King had given to his parliament, and
however acquiescent the official Church of England
might be in turning the other cheek, this state of affairs
could not endure. For the ninth Earl of Argyll landed in
Scotland with a handful of followers and tried to arouse
the ardour of the Presbyterians, while the Duke of Monmouth, the King's illegitimate nephew, pitched camp in
Lyme in Dorset, after sailing from Holland, and planned
to arouse the West of England and capture Bristol as a
base. Here, in fact, the dissenters rallied to the standard
of the "Protestant Duke" in large numbers. Crowds of
uncompromising nonconformist tradesmen and peasants
offered their services in the very area which had been most
persistently Royalist during the civil wars. The motives of
these men in joining Monmouth were religious and not
economic. The two rebellions came too soon and were
crushed. But noncomformity had been awakened out of its
passive acceptance of persecution by the old anti-papal
war-cries that had pierced the air in the sixteen-forties.
Soon the ruling classes were to unite almost solidly against
the Jesuit-inspired ambitions of King James II. Though
in his Declaration of Indulgence of 1687 the King tried to
draw over the nonconformists to his side, the Marquis of
Halifax, who had once been the protector of the rights
of James Stuart when his brother had been upon the
throne, riposted with a famous pamphlet, entitled *A Letter
to a Dissenter*, in which he argued that liberty and infalli-
bility were contradictory and that the nonconformists,
rather than trust the promises of the Declaration of

Indulgence, ought to await "the next probable revolution". When seven bishops were sent to the Tower of London to await trial for seditious libel because they had refused for specified reasons to permit the reading of King James II's second Declaration of Indulgence in the churches, many nonconformists actually assured them of their sympathy. Thus a virtually united nation drove the Roman Catholic King from his throne and achieved a revolution without a battle.

But if the nonconformists did not enter into conspiracies before the reign of King James II, there was a link between the men who had fought King Charles I and those who destroyed his son. A group of underground conspirators, some of whom had been imprisoned during the Clarendon régime, had emerged to associate, first with the second Duke of Buckingham whose "cabal" was said to include Cromwell's famous chaplain, Dr. John Owen, and caused Samuel Pepys to report : "Some say we are carried in Oliver's bucket." Later this group tried to exclude James Stuart from the throne and even to revive a republican movement. It was concerned in the so-called Rye House Plot (1683) against King Charles II, and later the Duke of Monmouth's rising. Some of these conspirators were caught and executed, but a few survivors fled to Holland and returned with William of Orange at the Glorious Revolution.

The Revolution Settlement in 1689 comprised an Act of Toleration which, in effect, acquiesced in organized nonconformity by permitting the suspension of the penal code against dissenting meetings and granting concessions to dissenting ministers. The Bill of Rights, to which King William III gave his assent in the same year, further reinforced the powers of parliament and reduced those of the Crown. It also laid it down that henceforward no monarch might be a Roman Catholic or marry a Roman Catholic. It was perhaps the greatest constitutional document in modern history and, like the revolution of 1649, it owed its origins to the misdeeds of a Stuart King.

After the pendulum had swung back in the early years of Charles II's reign, the settlement of 1689 thus completed the constitutional revolution of the seventeenth century. The Bill of Rights repaired some of the inadequacies of the legislation of 1641. Possibly if King Charles I had agreed to the same sort of restrictions upon his prerogative and if the parliamentary leaders could have trusted him, that settlement might have been attained earlier. As it was, the execution of King Charles I and the experiments of the Protectorate produced a Royalist reaction, but at the same time afforded a warning to the aristocracy and wealthier ruling classes of what might happen again if they did not this time join together to depose a monarch who attempted to dispense with parliament and rule by his personal powers. The importance of the Puritan Revolution in British history cannot be understood except in the context of the settlement in 1689.

It is sometimes said that this revolution was an historical aberation which it is best patriotically to slide over, an affront to the ideal of the peaceful and orderly constitutional progress which appeals to placid Englishmen. In the same way, Oliver Cromwell has never been accepted as a national hero in the same senses as, say, the first William Pitt, Earl of Chatham, the Duke of Wellington, or Lord Nelson. Not even a great soldier, some of his critics observe, for other men fought his battles for him, and anyhow he did not fight French or Germans but the Scots, the Irish, and his fellow countrymen. Disregarding the testimonies of his own letters and his own servants, his humaneness is denied because he treated the ancestors of the Sinn Feiners as badly as the Black-and-Tans. The Irish hate him because he conquered them, the Scots because he subdued them, the æsthetes because he collected horses instead of paintings, the Roman Catholics because he did not believe in the Mass, the Socialists because he suppressed the Levellers, the Liberals because for a short spell he ruled as a military dictator, the Conservatives because he killed a King.

But history need not be written in such simple terms, and Cromwell should be seen not through the coloured spectacles of our own emotions, but in the glaring light of his own times. One may conclude by quoting the words of a recent writer, not a professional historian but a detached observer :

"Cromwell's claim to greatness is that, within the limitations set him by the people he had to deal with and the events with which he had to contend, he pursued a policy which, apart from restoring our national reputation abroad, saved England at home from the extremes of bloody repression and deepening chaos.

"Cromwell neither betrayed, nor did he fulfil, the ideals of the Puritan Revolution. He tried and failed to make of Puritanism a political instrument. He was forced to acquiesce in an attempt, which failed, to impose upon England the Puritan pattern of social behaviour. But both these failures were contained within the frame of a larger success. A new principle of Government had been asserted; a new standard of behaviour had been established. For good or ill the religious and secular principles of the Reformation had been consolidated, and were never again to be seriously challenged. The defeat of James II had been assured thirty years before he ascended the throne; England had been secured from the Counter-Reformation, and from all its implications of bloodshed, misery and obscurantism."[1]

Thus the spirit and achievements of Oliver Cromwell were active elements in the revolution of 1688; they gave their impulse to a permanent form of English institutions; they largely attained their long-term objectives; and they may be said to have entered effectively into the making of modern England.

[1] John Marlowe, *The Puritan Tradition in English Life* (1956).

For Further Reading

Good biographies of Oliver Cromwell are *Oliver Cromwell and the Rule of the Puritans in England,* by Sir Charles Firth, revised in 1924, and *Oliver Cromwell,* by John Buchan, 1934. *The Greatness of Oliver Cromwell* (1957), by Maurice Ashley, aims to be a reasoned defence of the Lord Protector and to embody the results of historical research published since Firth's and Buchan's books appeared. The standard edition of the *Writings and Speeches of Oliver Cromwell* was completed by Wilbur Cortez Abbott in 1947, but *The Letters and Speeches of Oliver Cromwell,* by Thomas Carlyle, edited by S. C. Lomas in 1904, is still valuable and readable.

Dr. C. V. Wedgwood's *The Great Rebellion* is an up-to-date account of the Puritan Revolution, but greater detail will be found in S. R. Gardiner's *History of the Great Civil War* (1893), continued in his *History of the Commonwealth and Protectorate* (1903). This work was continued again by Sir Charles Firth in his *The Last Years of the Protectorate* (1909), and by Godfrey Davies in *The Restoration of King Charles II* (1955). Mr. David Ogg's *England in the Reign of Charles II* and *England in the Reigns of James II and William III* (1955) cover the political and social history of the remainder of the century. For a succinct account readers may perhaps be referred to *England in the Seventeenth Century* ("The Pelican History of England"), by Maurice Ashley, revised in 1958. For the social life of the Interregnum, F. A. Inderwick, *The Interregnum* (1891) is still useful, and there is *Social Policy during the Puritan Revolution* (1930), by Margaret James. Two very recent books to which reference is made in Chapter Fourteen are *Puritanism in the Period of the Great Persecution, 1660–1688,* by G. R. Cragg (1957), and *King and Commons, 1660–1832,* by Betty Kemp (1957).

Other recent books of special value for this period are : Paul H. Hardacre, *The Royalists during the Puritan Revolution* (1956), J. G. A. Pocock, *The Ancient Constitution and the Feudal Law* (1957), and George Yule, *The Independents in the Great Civil War* (1958).

For an up-to-date Marxist view of the period there is "Recent Interpretations of the Civil War", by Christopher Hill in *History*, Vol. LXI (1956), and *The Good Old Cause*, by Christopher Hill and Edmund Dell (1949). Mr. Hill believes that the "Puritan Revolution" was a nineteenth-century myth. For a Christian view there is an excellent biography of Cromwell entitled *The Lord Protector*, by the Rev. Robert S. Paul (1955).

I am indebted to Mr. H. G. Tibbutt for allowing me to see proofs of his edition of 'The Tower of London Letter—Book of Sir Lewis Dyve, 1646-1647' which appears in the 1958 volume of the publications of the Bedfordshire Records Socity of which I have made use in Chapter Six.

Index